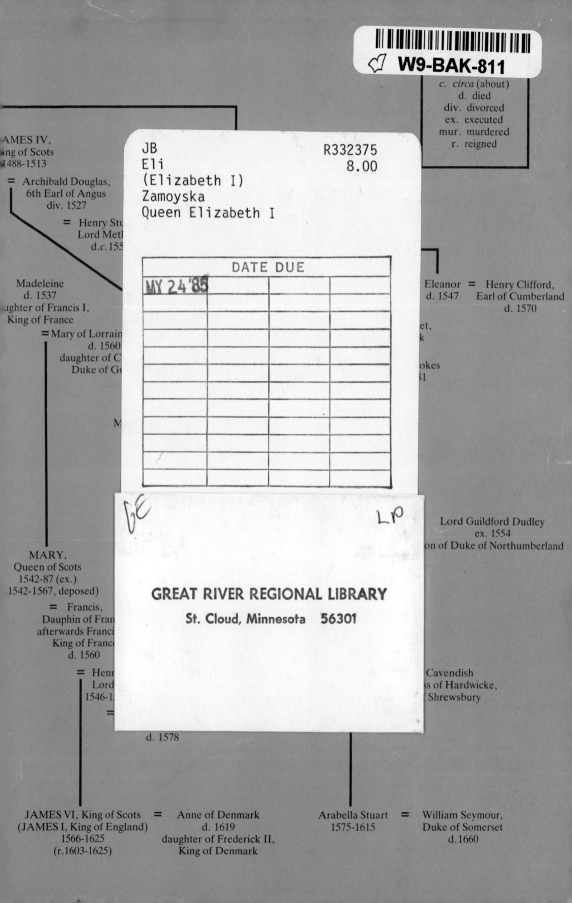

c. *circa* (about)
d. died
div. divorced
ex. executed
mur. murdered
r. reigned

[J]AMES IV,
[Ki]ng of Scots
[1]488-1513

= Archibald Douglas,
6th Earl of Angus
div. 1527

= Henry Stu...
Lord Meth...
d.c. 155...

Madeleine
d. 1537
[da]ughter of Francis I,
King of France

= Mary of Lorrain...
d. 1560
daughter of C...
Duke of Gu...

M...

Eleanor = Henry Clifford,
d. 1547    Earl of Cumberland
d. 1570

MARY,
Queen of Scots
1542-87 (ex.)
1542-1567, deposed)

= Francis,
Dauphin of Fran...
afterwards Franci...
King of France
d. 1560

= Henr...
Lord...
1546-1...

=

d. 1578

Lord Guildford Dudley
ex. 1554
...on of Duke of Northumberland

...Cavendish
...ss of Hardwicke,
...f Shrewsbury

JAMES VI, King of Scots = Anne of Denmark
(JAMES I, King of England)     d. 1619
1566-1625            daughter of Frederick II,
(r.1603-1625)             King of Denmark

Arabella Stuart = William Seymour,
1575-1615      Duke of Somerset
d.1660

First distribution in the United States of America by McGraw-Hill Book Company 1981.

Produced by Cameron & Tayleur (Books) Ltd

Series editors: Ian Cameron, Jill Hollis
Designed by Ian Cameron

Library of Congress Cataloging in Publication Data

Zamoyska, Betka.
    Queen Elizabeth I.

    (Leaders series)
    Includes index.
    SUMMARY: A biography of the daughter of Henry VIII, depicting not only her vulnerability as a human being, but her decisiveness as a queen whose policies changed England from a minor country into a world power.
    1. Elizabeth, Queen of England, 1533–1603—Juvenile literature.    2. Great Britain—History—Elizabeth, 1558–1603—Juvenile literature.    3. Great Britain—Kings and rulers—Biography—Juvenile literature.    [1. Elizabeth, Queen of England, 1533–1603.    2. Kings, queens, rulers, etc.    3. Great Britain—History—Elizabeth, 1558–1603]
I. Title.    II. Series.
DA355.Z35    1981        942.05'5'0924        80-28135
ISBN 0-07-072721-X        [B]    [92]

*Picture credits*
Reproduced by gracious permission of Her Majesty the Queen: 11a

The Marquess of Bath: 59a
Bibliothèque Nationale, Paris: 36b
Bodleian Library, Oxford: 52c
Trustees of the British Museum: 29; 30; 51; 66
By courtesy of the Earl of Bradford: 7a
Cooper-Bridgeman Library: cover; 4; 7b; 34; 35a; 56; 57; 66
Dept. of Environment, Edinburgh: 49
Drake Collection, Hants: 56
Reproduced by permission of the Syndics of the Fitzwilliam Museum, Cambridge: 33
Lauros-Giraudon, Paris: 36a
By courtesy of the Duke of Hamilton: 44
The Controller, HMSO: 42
Hever Castle Estate: 53a
Michael Holford Library: 6; 22a, b; 30; 51; 54
The Mansell Collection: 9b; 14; 17; 23; 24; 32; 40a; 50
Lord Methuen: 63
National Gallery of Ireland, Dublin: 59b
The National Maritime Museum, London: 52b; 54; 55
National Portrait Gallery, London: 9a; 10; 11b; 12; 13; 19; 20; 25; 27; 35b; 47; 52a; 53b; 59c
Prado Museum, Madrid: 22a, b
Picturepoint Ltd: 52c
The Public Record Office: 21
By courtesy of the Earl of Radnor: 57
By courtesy of the Marquess of Salisbury: cover; 66
Sherborne Castle Estates: 31
Society of Antiquaries: 12–13
Weidenfeld & Nicolson Archives: 7a; 21; 29; 36a; 36b; 38; 40; 42; 48; 49; 57; 59a, b; 63; 65

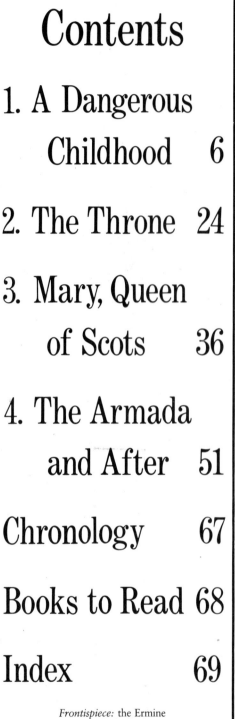

# Contents

*Frontispiece:* the Ermine Portrait of Elizabeth I by Nicholas Hilliard.

# Queen Elizabeth I

## BETKA ZAMOYSKA

## McGRAW-HILL BOOK COMPANY
### New York  St. Louis  San Francisco

# 1.    A Dangerous Childhood

The Tower of London, with old London Bridge in the background. From a manuscript of around 1500.

On Friday, May 19th, 1536, at eight o'clock in the morning, Anne Boleyn, the Queen, was brought to execution on the green within the Tower of London. The mother of the two-year-old Princess Elizabeth was to die at the order of Elizabeth's father, King Henry VIII of England. Anne Boleyn's death was observed by an anonymous Spaniard who was probably one of a group of spectators allowed in to watch the execution. He described Anne as being "as gay as if she was not going to die." She was wearing a night robe of damask with a red damask skirt and a netted coif (cap) over her hair, as befitted the occasion. The executioner asked Anne's forgiveness and begged her to kneel and say her prayers.

"So Anne knelt, but the poor lady only kept looking about her. The headsman, being still in front of her, said in French,

'Madam, do not fear, I will wait till you tell me.' Then she said, 'You will have to take this coif off,' and she pointed to it with her left hand. The sword was hidden under a heap of straw, and the man who was to give it to the headsman was told beforehand what to do; so, in order that she should not suspect, the headsman turned to the steps by which they had mounted, and called out, 'Bring me the sword.' The lady looked towards the steps to watch for the coming of the sword, still with her hand on her coif; and the headsman made a sign with his right hand for them to give him the sword, and then, without being noticed by the lady, he struck off her head to the ground.''

Anne Boleyn, a drawing by Hans Holbein.

Henry VIII by Hans Holbein.

It was a fittingly dramatic death for one who had helped to bring about great changes to the England of her time. In order to marry Anne, Henry VIII had broken with the Church of Rome, which, led by the Pope, held sway over the whole of Catholic Europe. He established the Church of England with himself as its head. Henry wanted a son and heir because he and Catherine of Aragon, his first wife, had only one surviving child, a daughter called Mary. Catherine was older than the King and nearly past the age of child-bearing when he first noticed the attractive Anne Boleyn at Court. Anne's older sister had been Henry's mistress, but Anne was shrewd enough to hold out for a more secure position. Henry was wilful and used to having his own way, so that when he realized Anne would not become his mistress, he was determined to marry her.

Catherine had first been married to Henry's older brother, Arthur, who died shortly after the wedding. Henry now declared that he had sinned against God's will in marrying his sister-in-law, which was why she had not borne him a son. He asked the Pope to annul his marriage. It was the Pope's refusal that led to Henry's founding the Church of England. He could then announce to his surprised subjects that his marriage had not been valid and that Catherine, the woman who had been Queen for 24 years, was not really his wife. He also declared that his daughter, Mary, was a bastard. The English people were shocked to hear the respectable Queen Catherine being dismissed as the King's concubine and even more horrified to learn that the scheming Lady Anne Boleyn was to become the new Queen. Anne finally gave in to Henry and became pregnant by him in order to hasten the marriage. She had been flirting with him for six years and by January 1533 she was becoming desperate. Henry married her in secret in order to ensure that his child was legitimate. On May 31st, she rode in state through the City of Westminster to be crowned. However, Anne Boleyn also produced a daughter, Elizabeth, who was born on September 7th, 1533. When her second child, a son, miscarried, she too fell from favor. Henry then turned his attention to Jane Seymour, a maid-of-honor in Anne's service, who was soon to become his third wife. History was repeating itself. Anne was conveniently found guilty of adultery and of plotting against the King. She was condemned to death for high treason.

Elizabeth, like Mary, was declared illegitimate. She was not yet three years old when she suffered the same loss of

Catherine of Aragon, Henry VIII's first wife, whom he was trying to divorce at the time this portrait was painted, around 1530.

Jane Seymour, Henry VIII's third wife, who died only twelve days after giving birth to his only son, the future Edward VI.

rank, but she is supposed to have remarked with displeasure about her change of title: "How haps it? Yesterday my Lady Princess, today but my Lady Elizabeth!"

No one knows how or when Elizabeth came to know of the circumstances of her mother's death but it is unlikely that she could have been kept in ignorance for long. In those days, the Court, the retinue of councillors and attendants who served the King and travelled around with him to his various palaces, was a tight-knit community where gossip flourished.

Mary and Elizabeth each had separate households, with retainers, cooks, servants and ladies-in-waiting to attend them. However, they often visited the same palaces together or met when they were asked to join the King at Court. Elizabeth was a precocious child, and her half-sister Mary wrote in a letter to their father: "My sister Elizabeth is such a child toward as I doubt not but your Highness shall have cause to rejoice in time to come."

Elizabeth's upbringing had its problems, but these were domestic ones which had little to do with Court politics. Margaret Bryan, the Lady Mistress or Governess of Elizabeth's household, complained to one of the King's ministers that Elizabeth "has neither gown nor kirtle nor petticoat, nor linene for smocks", and gave a long list of the many other necessities that her royal charge was without.

This neglect of Elizabeth was probably not intentional. After Anne's death, though, there were doubtless fewer people to represent her daughter's interests at Court. Anne's fall from favor had left Elizabeth and her household in an ambiguous position.

In the absence of any higher authority, the male head of the household, Mr. John Shelton, began to interfere in Elizabeth's upbringing and insisted that his three-year-old mistress dine in state, publicly. Lady Bryan wrote: "Mr. Shelton would have my lady Elizabeth to dine and sup every day at the board of estate. It is not meet for a child of her age to keep such rule yet. If she do, I dare not take it upon me to keep her Grace in health; for there she shall see divers meats; and fruits, and wine, which it would be hard for me to restrain her Grace from." It was a difficult age at which to preside gracefully over the dinner tables, especially as Elizabeth was having trouble with her teeth.

Jane Seymour, Henry's third wife, finally gave him the son he had so long waited for. On October 12th, 1537, Elizabeth's half brother, Edward, was born at the Palace of Hampton Court. Elizabeth, now four years old, took part in the ceremonial procession at his christening. Much of Elizabeth's time soon came to be spent with her younger brother. As they grew up together, they became very fond of each other. Since both were intelligent and studious, they had much in common. When Edward was six years old, he and Elizabeth shared the same tutors and did most of their lessons together.

Henry VIII, painted in about 1542.

Children in those days began their studies very early in the morning (often the moment it was light, at four or five o'clock in summertime). They were expected to work long hours, and the cane was used frequently on those who found other distractions. Elizabeth and Edward, with their ability for hard work and concentration, were lucky enough not to need it. Over the years, their tutors wrote glowing reports of their progress. Edward was writing Latin verses at the age of seven and, at ten, Elizabeth was excellent at Latin, and she could speak Italian well. As well as learning ancient and modern languages and being instructed in religion,

10

Henry VIII's three children, all destined to become monarchs. *Left:* Elizabeth in 1547, when she would have been fourteen. *Above:* Edward, around 1542, when he would have been five. *Right:* Mary, aged 27, in 1544.

which formed the major part of her education, she studied history, geography, mathematics, science and music.

As she grew older, Elizabeth was tutored on her own. She was fortunate enough to be taught by some of the most talented and interesting scholars of the day, such as William Grindall and Roger Ascham. Ascham was justifiably proud of his royal pupil. When she was sixteen, he wrote to a friend that Elizabeth had the gifts of "beauty, stature, prudence, and industry." He reported that: "Her study of true religion and learning is most eager. Her mind has no womanly weakness, her perseverance is equal to that of a man, and her memory long keeps what it quickly picks up. She talks French and Italian as well as she does English, and has often talked to me readily and well in Latin, moderately in Greek. When she writes Greek and Latin, nothing is more beautiful than her handwriting. She delights as much in music as she is skilful in it."

Elizabeth kept up her studies even when she became Queen. She often used to read Greek and Latin with Ascham as a distraction from the endless round of State papers and duties. At the time, Latin was a common language among educated Europeans and literature and poetry were still widely read in either Latin or Greek.

In addition to her studies, Elizabeth had other pleasures. She loved dancing, hunting, hawking and taking walks

through the elaborate gardens and fine parks that surrounded the royal palaces. Throughout her life, Elizabeth enjoyed taking exercise and, as a child, she was exceptionally healthy, unlike her younger brother, Edward. She suffered from few of the diseases that then often killed young children.

*Edward becomes King*

The peaceful period that the two children enjoyed together was not to last. At the end of November 1546, Edward and Elizabeth were separated. Edward, who was sent with his entourage to Hertford Castle, wrote a pathetic letter in Latin to his sister at the palace at Enfield, Middlesex.

"The change of place," he wrote, "in fact, did not vex me so much, dearest sister, as your going from me. Now, however, nothing can happen more agreeable to me than a letter from you; and especially as you were the first to send a letter to me and have challenged me to write. Wherefore I thank you both for your good-will and despatch . . . But this is some comfort to my grief, that I hope to visit you shortly (if no accident intervene with either me or you), as my chamberlain has reported to me."

The coronation procession of Edward VI passing through the streets of London.

Shortly, however, there was to be a dramatic change in the lives of both children. When they met again at Enfield, two months after that letter was written, Edward's uncle, Edward Seymour, Earl of Hertford, broke the news to them that their father, Henry VIII, had died. The fair, delicate little boy and the red-headed girl clung together weeping.

Unlike their older half sister, Mary, neither Edward nor Elizabeth had suffered directly from the cruel and ruthless streak in Henry's nature. Henry had originally been fond of Mary, but her determination to remain a Roman Catholic and to stand by her mother infuriated him, and he began to treat her harshly. During Anne Boleyn's brief heyday, Mary was sent to wait on Elizabeth, who was given preference over her and made her social superior. Edward and Elizabeth had seen their father only on special occasions, when they were brought to Court or when he came to visit his country palaces. They had admired his impressive, regal stature, his charm, his joviality, his fine clothes and his huge bodily presence. To Elizabeth and Edward he was exactly what a great king should be. While he lived, both children knew

13

that they were under his protection. Now, as orphans, they would have to make their own way in a harsh world.

Edward Seymour, Earl of Hertford, became the guardian of his ten-year-old nephew, who was now King Edward VI. Seymour had become Lord Protector of England, and was thus in charge of the kingdom while the King was too young to take on the full responsibilities of a ruling sovereign. Henry VIII's sixth and last wife, Catherine Parr, was given charge of Elizabeth, who was now thirteen and a half.

While Edward struggled with the rivalries of the powerful nobles at his Court, Elizabeth became involved in her first serious political crisis. Edward Seymour had a good-looking, ambitious younger brother called Thomas who envied his position and was determined to increase his own power. He first planned to marry one of the royal princesses, Elizabeth or Mary, but he realized that he would never get the agreement of his brother or of the Privy Council, the King's permanent advisers on matters of state. So instead he decided to marry the King's widow, the 34-year-old Queen Catherine Parr, who had always been fond of him. After the wedding, Elizabeth found herself in the care not only of her stepmother Catherine, but also of a tawny-headed, rambunctious stepfather of 38 with a great reputation for womanizing. She soon discovered that her new stepfather's attentions were rather more than paternal. It was later reported that he would "come many mornings into the Lady Elizabeth's chamber, before she were ready, and sometimes before she did rise. And if she were up, he would bid her good morrow, and ask how she did, and strike her upon the back or on the buttocks familiarly, and so go forth through his lodgings."

Edward Seymour, Earl of Hertford and later Duke of Somerset, Lord Protector of England after Edward VI came to the throne. He died in 1552. Picture engraved from a painting by Holbein.

Sometimes he was even known to pull back the curtains that hung around the four poster bed and "make as though he would come at her," but his wary stepdaughter would "go further into the bed, so that he could not come at her." He once tried to kiss her in bed, but luckily Elizabeth's governess, Kat Ashley, was present and sent him packing. Elizabeth was in a difficult position because she was very fond of her stepmother, who was one of the few people left to help and protect her. Catherine had always been kind to her and had taken pains to see that she, like her brother Edward, was instructed in the Anglican faith of the Church of England.

Elizabeth had no wish to offend Catherine, but was flattered by her stepfather's attentions. His high spirits must

Catherine Parr, the sixth wife of Henry VIII, who was given charge of Elizabeth after the death of the King. This picture was painted around 1545 and uses an old spelling of her name.

KATHARINE PARRE

have made a welcome change after the carefully regulated training of her early years. To avoid further bedroom scenes, Elizabeth began getting up very early so that when Seymour in his nightgown came bounding in she would be sitting fully dressed, primly reading a book.

Rather unwisely, Catherine sometimes took part in her husband's antics. She once held Elizabeth captive while Seymour "cut her gown into an hundred pieces." Yet however much Catherine pretended that these games were all in fun, tensions inevitably began to arise between the older woman and her teenage stepdaughter. Matters eventually came to a head when Catherine, who was by then pregnant, discovered her husband and Elizabeth in an embrace. Catherine, hurt and angry, was also seriously alarmed. If a royal virgin was found in a compromising position, it was a serious matter both for herself and her guardians. Catherine hurriedly arranged for Elizabeth and her household to move to

Theobald's Palace, near Cheshunt in Hertfordshire, the week after Whitsun, 1548. From here, Elizabeth wrote her stepmother a sad, apologetic little note which shows that she was not entirely innocent in the whole affair:

"Although I could not be plentiful in giving thanks for the manifold kindness received at your Highness' hand at my departure, yet I am something to be borne withal, for truly I was replete with sorrow to depart from your Highness, especially leaving you undoubtful of health: and, albeit I answered little, I weighed it more deeper, when you said you would warn me of all evils that you should hear of me; for if your Grace had not a good opinion of me, you would not have offered friendship to me that way, that all men judge the contrary."

Catherine had evidently scolded Elizabeth for her conduct and warned her of the hazards of her position. Elizabeth was second in line to the throne after her stepsister Mary; she could not afford to have a tainted reputation. People had not forgotten that Elizabeth's mother, Anne Boleyn, had been accused of adultery and immoral behavior.

This was the last advice Elizabeth was to receive from her stepmother. On September 5th, 1548 Catherine died, shortly after the birth of her child. Another girl who had been in Catherine's care, the ten-year-old Lady Jane Grey, was chief mourner at the burial service. Lady Jane, who was outstandingly intelligent and well-educated, was destined to play a historic role in the events of her country.

After his wife's death, Seymour began to take an active interest in Elizabeth's property and he questioned her steward or cofferer, Thomas Parry, about her inheritance. When Elizabeth heard about this and asked Parry the reason for Seymour's interest, Parry answered: "I do not know unless he would like to have you also." Elizabeth found herself the center of romantic speculation and, although she realized the dangers of this, she could not stop the gossip around her. Her sentimental governess, Kat Ashley, enjoyed talking about Seymour and encouraging Elizabeth's interest in him.

Seymour had started openly canvassing support to oust his brother from power and thereby put an end to the Protectorate. He also became involved in dubious financial dealings in order to raise money quickly, probably with a view to paying for an army. Eventually reports of his "disloyal practices" grew to such a pitch that the Privy Council held a meeting on January 17th, 1549, when they unanimously decided "to commit the said Admiral to prison in the Tower of London, there to remain till such further order be taken with him as the case . . . shall require."

Seymour's intrigues to marry Elizabeth had also come to light. Mrs. Ashley and Thomas Parry were committed to the Tower for questioning; Elizabeth's household was then at Hatfield Palace in Hertfordshire, and Sir Robert Tyrwhitt was sent to interrogate her. Tyrwhitt tried to persuade her to speak out by saying that the blame would be laid on her governess and Thomas Parry, but he had not taken into account their young mistress's strong sense of loyalty. Tyrwhitt was surprised to find himself losing a battle of wits with this determined young girl of sixteen. Elizabeth was walking a dangerous tightrope and she knew it. In spite of all Tyrwhitt's efforts, she outwitted him at every turn, refusing to confess to anything that could be used against her.

Parry was not so strong a personality. After a week of questioning, he told all that is now known about Elizabeth's relations with Seymour and his interest in her property. Confronted with this confession, Kat Ashley also gave in and signed a joint confession which was sent to Elizabeth. When confronted with it, Elizabeth was reported to be "much abashed and half breathless ere she could read it to an end". As a king's daughter, it must have been embarrassing to see descriptions of Seymour's bottom-slapping flirtation written down for all to read. Yet she was quick to realize that neither Parry nor Kat Ashley implied that she had taken an active part in Seymour's marriage schemes, nor could she be accused of taking any part in his treasonable activities. The worst of the crisis was over. Elizabeth was given another governess to replace Kat Ashley, but she opposed the change so strongly that both Parry and Kat Ashley were eventually returned to her.

Elizabeth had come through her first serious political dilemma triumphant and outwardly unscathed. Seymour, however, was executed on March 20th, 1549. On hearing of his death, Elizabeth is said to have remarked: "There died a man with much wit and very little judgment." It may seem a callous comment for a young girl to make about her first suitor, but then the man's lack of judgment could have cost her her own head as well.

She was learning fast that emotions had to take second place in the dangerous political struggle for survival. In her subsequent relationships with men, she was gay and flirtatious on the surface but remained wary underneath. She had come to realize, at a very young age, the dangers of personal

Thomas, Lord Seymour of Sudeley, the brother of the Lord Protector, Edward Seymour, and husband of Catherine Parr. Picture engraved from a painting by Holbein.

commitments. To help extinguish any trace of scandal, Elizabeth took to dressing and behaving in an exceptionally demure manner and once more applied herself to her studies. She took care to keep well out of all the remaining intrigues of her brother's reign. The Lord Protector, Edward Seymour, by now Duke of Somerset, fell from power, and the Earl of Northumberland took his place, but Elizabeth remained unscathed.

*Lady Jane Grey and Mary I*

By May 1553, it became evident that Edward, who had been ailing for some time, was now fatally ill. The constant stress of political intrigue must have added to the trials of the nervous, sickly boy. As early as 1552, a year before his death, the Earl of Northumberland was making plans to tamper with the Act of Succession made by Henry VIII. This decreed that if Edward died childless, Mary, Henry's oldest daughter, should succeed to the throne. If she also died without children, the crown was to pass to Elizabeth. Northumberland persuaded Edward to pass over both Mary's and Elizabeth's claims in his will and to make his cousin, Lady Jane Grey, the next in line to the throne. Against her will, the fifteen-year-old Lady Jane was married to one of Northumberland's sons, Guildford Dudley. By this means, Northumberland hoped to maintain his own position after Edward's death.

On July 4th, 1553, Northumberland summoned Mary and Elizabeth to their half brother's deathbed. Mary discovered it was a trap, broke her journey and fled to Framlingham in Suffolk. Elizabeth said she was too ill to travel and wisely retired to bed. When Mary learned of Northumberland's plot to seize the throne for Lady Jane Grey she moved to Norfolk, where many people, angry at Northumberland's high-handedness, came to her support. It was commonly known that Henry VIII had arranged for his daughter to be next in line and the people were not prepared to accept an impostor as their Queen. Although Mary set out with only a handful of supporters, an army was soon mustered to take up her cause. Northumberland was forced to back down, and Mary was proclaimed Queen. As a devout Catholic, she believed that God had brought about her victory so that she could restore England to the Roman Catholic faith.

As soon as Elizabeth heard of her sister's victory, she wrote to congratulate her. Then she set out to join Mary on her triumphant way to London. The two sisters arrived in the capital together. They made a striking contrast. Mary,

Lady Jane Grey, who was named in Edward VI's will as next in line of succession to the throne, a reluctant Queen who was executed at the age of seventeen.

now 37, was thin and worn down by worry and harassment. Standing by her mother throughout her parents' separation, Mary had refused to comply with Henry's demands that she should acknowledge that her mother's marriage was invalid. She would not accept that she was illegitimate or recognize the new Church of England. She clung bravely to Roman Catholicism throughout her father's reign and withstood the constant persecutions of Edward's Protestant ministers. All these trials had turned Mary into an embittered, religious bigot.

Elizabeth, at twenty years of age, appeared to be in the full bloom of life. She was quite tall with a good figure and moved with great dignity. Her hair was reddish-gold and she had an olive complexion. Her features were striking: she had fine eyes and long, elegant hands, of which she was particularly proud. Having been brought up in the new religion like most of her generation, she looked upon the Roman Catholic faith as a strange, foreign ritual and had no knowledge of its doctrines or beliefs. Soon after her accession, Mary set about establishing Roman Catholicism as the national faith and Elizabeth had to conform.

Elizabeth was well skilled in the arts of survival and, as next in line to the throne, was not going to jeopardize her chances for the future. Hers was the difficult task of having to conform openly to Catholicism while at the same time keeping the support of the Protestants and the younger generation who looked upon her as their one hope for the future. She let it be assumed that she was constrained to become a Catholic by force and that her real sympathies were still with the Protestants, but was careful to confide in no one. Although Mary suspected that Elizabeth was being insincere, she had no proof, and Elizabeth took every opportunity to demonstrate that she was an obedient, loving and respectful sister. She knew how keen her enemies would be to brand her as a heretic and a traitor.

In 1554, the second year of her reign, Mary, whose mother was Spanish, began negotiations to marry Philip II of Spain. The English people were horrified at the idea. Spain and France were the two greatest powers in Europe. The English saw themselves becoming a tiny part of the Spanish dominions and being drawn into expensive Spanish wars against France. Mary was also determined to restore the Pope's authority in England. The people began to foresee the unwelcome possibility of foreign interference in all their affairs. After Mary's marriage negotiations became public, wild rumors spread throughout the country about the wicked habits of the Spaniards and the cruel persecution of heretics. A rebellion was planned, and a Kentish squire, Sir Thomas Wyatt, with his followers, marched into London in January 1554. They hoped to oust Mary and her Catholic supporters from power and to put Elizabeth on the throne in her place. Wyatt was defeated and executed and many of his followers were hanged. Up to this time, Mary had shown clemency to Lady Jane Grey, who had been forced against her will to usurp the throne after Edward's death. Now Mary decided she could not spare any rival claimant to the throne and Lady Jane was executed at the age of seventeen.

Elizabeth had carefully avoided taking any part in the rebellion but was still inevitably one of the chief suspects. She was imprisoned in the Tower and interrogated. Fully aware of her danger, she took care to arouse as much public support as possible. She had always been popular with the people of London and knew that their support was one of her few remaining strengths. On the steps of the Traitors' Stairs, leading up to the Tower, she turned towards the sympathetic onlookers and declared: "Oh Lord! I never thought to have come in here as prisoner; and I pray you

Sir Thomas Wyatt, who was executed for leading a rebellion against Mary.

counselors yea and that afore J go to the tower (if it
be possible) if not afor J be further condemned · howbeit J
trust assuredly your highnes wyl giue me leue to do it afor
J be thus shamfully J may not be cried out on as now J shal
be yea and without cause · let conciens moue your highnes to
take some bettar way with me tha to make me be condemned
in al mens sigth afor my desert knowen · Also J most humbly
beseche your highnes to pardon · this my boldnes wiche
innocecy procures me to do toogither with hope of your natural
kindnis wiche J trust wyl not se me cast away without desert
wiche what it is J wold desier no more of God but that you

all, good friends and fellows, bear me witness that I come
in no traitor but as true a woman to the Queen's Majesty
as any is now living; and thereupon will I take my death."

In spite of the careful examination of Elizabeth and many
other witnesses, the Government could find no proof of her
treachery. Elizabeth had not communicated with the rebels
or given any sign of support. Eventually she was released
from the Tower and sent to live, under close surveillance, in
the manor of Woodstock in Oxfordshire. She found this
semi-imprisonment irksome, but at least the worst danger
was over.

After Mary's marriage to Philip of Spain, Elizabeth found
herself in a better position. Philip was worried that Elizabeth's first cousin, Mary, Queen of Scots, who was married
to the son of the French king, might claim the English
throne. If she did so, she would have the backing of France,
Spain's worst enemy. Philip preferred Elizabeth's claim to
that of her Scottish cousin, so did not want Elizabeth to be
treated as a traitor. She was brought to Court where she
soon got herself into Philip's good graces. In October 1555,
she was sent back to Hatfield Palace where she stayed for
most of the remaining years of her sister's reign. She returned
to much the same routine as she had had as a young girl
with her tutor, Ascham.

There were still occasional anxieties. Another plot against
Mary, the Dudley plot, created a disturbance in Elizabeth's
household when some of her servants were implicated. Although Elizabeth was not officially suspected, she was placed
under the guardianship of Sir Thomas Pope in case she
became mixed up in any future conspiracy. Sir Thomas was

Philip II of Spain and his wife, Mary I of England. Paintings by Antonio Moro from the Prado Gallery, Madrid.

a cultured, entertaining man and he and Elizabeth enjoyed each other's company. During Shrovetide, 1556, he presented Elizabeth with a masque in the Great Hall at Hatfield. The masque combined music and drama, with twelve minstrels and knights and ladies, all dressed in elaborate and beautiful costumes. The festivities, which included a banquet of 70 dishes, lasted for two days. Mary wrote angrily to the Pope about these amusements but, when she visited her sister the following year, she did not object to the lavish entertainments laid on for her benefit. These included bear-baiting, a play and some fine singing for which Elizabeth provided the accompaniment, playing on the virginals. It was the last time the sisters met. Within a year, Mary was dying.

Her reign, which had begun so propitiously, ended in the horror of religious persecution. Many Protestants, as the adherents of the new faith were now called, refused to be converted to Roman Catholicism. They were treated as heretics and burned at the stake in public places to discourage others from following their example. Hundreds of Protestants showed such courage during the agonies of dying in slow-burning fires that they came to be revered as martyrs. Mary, who had once been so popular, was loathed and feared by her people. Her husband, Philip, left her to rule alone for most of her reign while he attended to his own affairs abroad. He involved the English in the Spanish war with France, in which England lost Calais, her only territory abroad. By the end of Mary's reign the Treasury was almost bankrupt. As Mary was childless, she had to accept the bitter fact that Elizabeth, whom she knew to be Protestant at heart, was going to succeed her. Her plans to return England to the Church of Rome and to produce a Catholic heir had failed.

As she lay dying, a sick, embittered woman, she probably heard that the roads to Hatfield Palace were crowded with important dignitaries rushing to pay court to their future Queen. The English people's hopes and interests were now centered on the 25-year-old girl, who was of English parentage and of Protestant upbringing.

Nicholas Ridley, Bishop of London, and Hugh Latimer, formerly Bishop of Worcester, were burned at the stake for heresy at Oxford in 1555. One of the many such executions recorded in Foxe's *Book of Martyrs*, first published in 1563 (this picture is from the 1632 edition).

🙚 A table deſcribing the burning of Biſhop Ridley and Father Latimer at Oxford, D.Smith there preaching at the time of their martirdome.

# 2.

# The Throne

On a mild afternoon in November 1558, Elizabeth was sitting under an oak tree in the park at Hatfield reading the Greek Testament. She looked up to see a cavalcade of horsemen approaching. The Lords of the Council were coming to tell her that she was Queen. On hearing what they had to say, she promptly got up and knelt on the grass, saying out loud: "It is the Lord's doing and marvellous in our eyes."

Elizabeth seldom made a mistake in her public performances. She had probably considered with care how she would react to news she had been expecting for several months. Her humble act of thanksgiving emphasized to her new subjects that she was God's chosen vessel, the instrument through which His people were to be ruled. Their new Queen, who had been declared illegitimate by her father and whose mother had been described as a whore, was determined to show that she was God's anointed. By now, Elizabeth had learned very well how to cope with the precariousness of her position. She had been a suspect and a prisoner and had seen how short a step it was from the throne to the block.

From her mother, Anne Boleyn, Elizabeth had inherited a sharp tongue, foresight and wiliness, and from her father, Henry VIII, her red-gold hair, physical energy, self-confidence, family pride, vanity, personal magnetism and sound political instinct. She also had the ability of her grandfather, Henry VII, to appreciate the value of money and to be cold and calculating in matters of statecraft. Altogether, she was a formidable young woman.

She knew how to assert her authority. Philip II's envoy, the Count de Feria, sent from Spain to report back on matters of state in England, disliked and distrusted Elizabeth. He reported that: "She seems to me incomparably more feared than her sister, and gives her orders and has her way as absolutely as her father did."

This comment would probably have delighted the new Tudor queen. She wanted to establish the same imperious presence that people had so admired in her father. The fact that she succeeded, in spite of being a woman, was an added triumph. Women rulers had a difficult task in the 16th century. The Scottish preacher, John Knox, had published a pamphlet at the time of Elizabeth's accession in which he asserted that it was against the natural order of things for

John Knox, the Scottish preacher.

women to rule over men. Women were considered to be inferior to men and they were brought up to believe that when they became wives, they should obey their husbands in all things. The English people expected that their young Queen would soon marry a suitable man who could take over the affairs of state and leave her to become a royal wife and mother. Philip II of Spain wrote that Elizabeth must find a husband "to relieve her of those labors which are only fit for men." However, she was in no hurry to marry and soon had the affairs of state well under her control.

Mary's reign had shown Elizabeth the dangers of making radical changes too quickly. She moved with extreme caution and took care to appoint advisers on whom she could rely. She turned to the forward-thinking group of Cambridge graduates that included her tutors, Ascham and Grindal. They were Protestants, full of the new ideas of their age.

The most important of these men was Sir William Cecil. Like many of the most influential men in Elizabeth's government, he was not a nobleman. His grandfather had been

William Cecil, Principal Secretary to Elizabeth and the most important of her advisers. In 1571, he was created Lord Burghley. He died in 1598.

the younger son of a poor Welsh squire and the family had only become important under the Tudors. At 38, William Cecil had survived all the political changes of the two previous reigns and, though a convinced Protestant, he had conformed under Mary. He was a man of intellect rather than emotion and, like Elizabeth, he had undergone a hard training in diplomacy and statecraft. Within a few days of her succession, Elizabeth appointed him her Principal Secretary and, after the official period of mourning was over, she had him sworn in as a member of her Council. Elizabeth was a good judge of people. Cecil proved to be more than worthy of the trust she placed in him and they had a long and successful working partnership that lasted for most of her reign. She had little time for flatterers and preferred people with sufficient intelligence and integrity to speak their own minds. "This judgment I have of you," she said to Cecil, "that you will not be corrupted with any manner of gift, and that you will be faithful to the State, and that without respect of my private will you will give me that counsel that you think best." Elizabeth delayed announcing most of the positions on her Council until she felt that her own position was more secure. She was determined to have a small, manageable Council in which professional experience and efficiency were the dominant factors. Elizabeth differed fundamentally from Mary in choosing laymen, not churchmen. She did not want either Protestant or Catholic extremists and, after careful consideration, she established a Council that blended the old with the new. The Council retained some of the important and influential nobles in the land in order to maintain the social order, and also included professional administrators, financial lawyers, men with outstanding military reputations and loyal supporters of her family.

The young Queen was equally cautious about changes in religion. She did not want Catholics stirring up trouble before she felt she had the solid support of the country behind her. Unlike Mary, Elizabeth was not fanatical. All that she expected from her subjects was outward conformity in religious matters. She began gradually to re-establish the Anglican faith that had been originated under her father and had become more fully established during her brother Edward's reign, when the first English Prayer Book was published. Elizabeth did not want to antagonize the Catholics as her sister had done with the Protestants. Characteristically, she settled for a compromise. She wanted the country

Elizabeth with the symbols of the monarchy: the crown, orb and scepter.

united by a national religion to which all except the extremists could conform. She broke with the Pope and the Latin Mass but retained the old order of priests and bishops. She also arranged for a second translation of the Prayer Book, which allowed for as wide an interpretation of Christian beliefs as possible so that Catholics and Protestants could adapt to it without offending against their own doctrines.

The other major problem for Elizabeth was the question of finance. Mary had left the country more or less bankrupt, and her sister knew that she could do little until the economy was on a stable basis.

Mary's reign had shown how disruptive and expensive wars could be to a small country. Throughout her life, Elizabeth tried to keep England out of them. She resolved to make her country the small but influential power that other great nations, particularly France and Spain, would woo for support against each other. This policy proved most effective, especially as Elizabeth, an unmarried woman, could herself be wooed by all the most important princes in Europe. She set about disentangling her country from the war with France so that England could be left in the strong position of being officially neutral. She never succeeded in regaining Calais, which Mary had lost, but, in the peace treaty of Cateau-Cambrésis, concluded on April 2nd, 1559, Calais was nominally left in English possession although it was in the temporary custody of France. Elizabeth had achieved another face-saving compromise. In reality, Calais was still in the hands of the French but at least the treaty brought an end to an expensive foreign war.

At home, with the help of William Cecil and her other financial advisers, she concentrated on making the country solvent. The silver coinage that had been debased with other metals during Mary's reign was called in and reissued, so that the money was restored to its real value in precious metal. By making strict economies, the government curbed inflation and gradually reduced the national debt. Elizabeth also saw to it that the administration of the towns became more centralized, so that her government could help to boost industry and encourage new crafts in areas where there was severe unemployment. With moderation, compromise and efficient administration, Elizabeth and her government gradually made the country more stable and prosperous.

*Elizabeth's coronation*

Elizabeth wanted to ward off the threats of greedy foreign powers, who saw England as a useful addition to their dominions. She was determined that her small realm should be considered one of the most important countries in Europe. Her sense of showmanship was invaluable in these schemes. She knew how important it was to set herself up as a beautiful and brilliant queen presiding over a glittering and cultured court. Her first big public performance was her coronation and Elizabeth saw to it that this was a glorious affair. A regiment of seamstresses, carters, saddlers and carpenters worked for over a month on the preparations. 700 yards (630 meters) of blue carpeting were provided for the Queen's procession through Westminster Abbey. The sum of £5,794 was spent on scarlet costumes for her household, and clothes for important officials of state cost a further £3,958. Altogether, Elizabeth spent £16,741.19s.8¾d. on the ceremony. The exactness of the sum shows how carefully she kept track of her expenses.

The date of Sunday, January 15th, 1559 was chosen for the coronation ceremony by the Astronomer Royal, Dr. John Dee, who cast the Queen's horoscope and observed the stars to discover the most propitious day for this event. On the Thursday before the coronation, Elizabeth sailed on the Thames from the palace in Whitehall to the Tower of London, where most royal sovereigns stayed before their coronations. On Saturday, there was the great coronation procession through the streets of London. In the morning, the whole Court assembled at the Tower and at two o'clock in the afternoon the Queen, carried in an open litter trimmed with gold brocade, set out to meet her new subjects. She was followed by a cavalcade of about a thousand people on horseback. The whole procession slowly made its way through the streets, past crowds of onlookers, to Westminster. The Queen was dressed in a robe of rich, gold cloth and she wore on her head the crown of a princess, as yet without the emblems of sovereignty. Her litter was drawn by two mules, also covered in gold draperies. On either side of her walked the gentlemen pensioners in crimson damask, bearing gilt battle-axes, and a great many footmen in crimson velvet jerkins, studded with silver gilt, and ornamented back and front with a white and red rose and the initials E. R., which stood for *Elizabeth Regina*, or Queen Elizabeth.

A contemporary sketch of the coronation procession of Elizabeth I

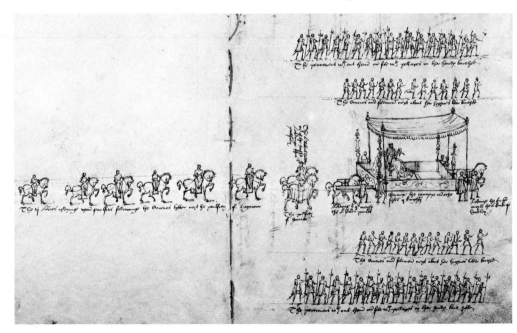

It was a cold, snowy day but everywhere the Queen was greeted with "prayers, wishes, welcomings, cries, tender words and all other signs which argued a wonderful and earnest love of most obedient subjects towards their Sovereign." Elizabeth showed her appreciation "by holding up her hands and merry countenance to such as stood far off, and by most tender and gentle language to those that stood nigh unto her Grace, did declare herself no less thankfully to receive her people's good will than they lovingly offered it unto her." All along the royal route there were pageants, presentations and speeches in Latin and English. Elizabeth took care to take special notice of the poor and humble. As one chronicler recounted: "How oftentimes stayed she her chariot when she saw any simple body offer to speak to her Grace?" Elizabeth knew how important it was to gain the love and support of ordinary people.

The following day Elizabeth was crowned in Westminster Abbey with full pomp and glory. As she was presented to the people for their acceptance, there was such shouting and noise of organs, fifes, trumpets, drums and bells that it seemed to one observer as though the world had come to an end. After the ceremony, the procession, led by Elizabeth

30

in full regalia, carrying the scepter and orb, returned to the Palace of Westminster for a long and stately feast. The spontaneous and warm way in which she greeted the cheering crowds won the people's hearts.

## Elizabeth's Court

Having won over her people, Elizabeth next had to establish herself at her Court. Being young and unmarried presented her with some awkward problems. All the courtiers were men, apart from a few ladies-in-waiting. Elizabeth therefore found herself in an almost entirely male society, as married courtiers usually left their wives at home to manage their estates. The young Queen had to keep the Court in order and maintain the spotless reputation that befitted a virgin queen. At the same time she had to make it sufficiently dazzling to attract important men to it.

Elizabeth created a myth around herself based on the old stories of chivalry, in which gallant knights in armor rushed to the aid of pure maidens. In her court, she became the virgin maid and her courtiers were her knights. They paid her homage and by acting out this role of the Virgin Queen, Elizabeth charmed her courtiers into subservience. She expected a high standard of "courtesy" from all who were

Queen Elizabeth being carried in procession. Most pictures of Elizabeth show little evidence of her true age – this one probably dates from late in her reign, when she was in her fifties or sixties.

admitted to her presence. Poets and composers praised her in their works, and immortalized her in the guises of Fair Oriana, Cynthia, the Moon goddess, or a beautiful shepherdess. These and many other descriptions of the Virgin Queen developed into a cult at her Court and made her famous throughout Europe. This cult continued into her old age, reaching a peak when she was about sixty.

Elizabeth enjoyed musical entertainments, masques and dramatic performances. Her Court became an important center for playwrights, poets, musicians and composers. Her reign was a time of great creativity, in which the arts flourished. Edmund Spenser, William Shakespeare and William Byrd are some of the greatest names of the age whose works are still appreciated. Spenser's poem, *The Faerie Queene*, represents Elizabeth as the fair maiden defended by her gallant knights. Shakespeare's history plays reflect the new sense of national pride that was engendered by Elizabeth. Her subjects were becoming interested in their past and proud of their heritage.

Hawking was a popular Tudor sport. This engraving of Elizabeth hawking is from a contemporary book, Turberville's *Book of Falconry*.

A Tudor palace, Nonesuch in Surrey, started under Henry VIII in 1538 and seen here in an early 17th-century painting. It was eventually demolished around 1670. Other palaces near London were at Greenwich and Richmond.

Elizabeth was also keen on sports and exercise. To keep herself fit, she would dance a lively dance, the galliard, in the mornings during intervals in state business. She also took frequent walks in her gardens and enjoyed hunting. She rode a great deal, as the Court moved from palace to palace. During the summer she also went on progresses, official tours, in the course of which she visited the great houses of nobles in the country both in order to avoid the risk of diseases in London and to make herself known to her subjects in different parts of her realm. Sometimes she travelled in a carriage, but when it was fine she would quite often set out on horseback and ride 10–20 miles (16–32 kilometers) in a day.

*Robert Dudley*

Elizabeth liked her courtiers to be fond of both intellectual and outdoor pursuits. She had been brought up by her tutors to appreciate the ideal of the "whole man" who was well educated and cultured but also adept at fencing, dancing, conversing, and behaving in a courtly manner. The men of action that Elizabeth loved and admired throughout her life almost always fitted this description. The man who first attracted her attention soon after she became Queen had all these qualities. He was Lord Robert Dudley, the son of the treacherous Duke of Northumberland.

At a time when a great many foreign princes were paying court to her, Elizabeth became involved in a scandal that might have ruined all her marriage prospects and threatened the sovereignty she had fought so hard to claim. At 26, Lord

33

Robert was about a year older than the Queen. He was tall,
good-looking, athletic and gallant; he was also known to be
popular with the women of the Court. Elizabeth made him
Master of the Horse and thus responsible for the care and
training of all the royal horses. As Elizabeth was a keen
horsewoman, they spent a lot of time together. It soon
became obvious to everyone at Court that Dudley was involved in a flirtation with the young Queen. However, Lord
Robert had been married since the age of seventeen. His
wife, Amy Robsart, who was ill, probably suffering from
cancer of the breast, was left alone at their house in the
country while Dudley was busy flirting with Elizabeth at
Court. The Queen became so obsessed with her elegant
suitor that the Duke of Norfolk, the chief peer of the realm,
complained of her "lightness and bad government." She
seemed to lose all interest in state business and the caution
she had shown throughout her girlhood was abandoned.

Cecil became so disturbed by Dudley's influence over the
Queen that he thought of retiring from Court. Many of the
Queen's chief ministers believed that Elizabeth was intent
on marriage. Cecil confided to the Spanish ambassador that
he feared that Dudley might even go so far as to kill his
wife. On the very day that Cecil voiced these fears, on
September 8th, 1560, Lady Dudley was found with a broken
neck at the foot of the stairs in her house, Cumnor Place,
near Oxford. All her servants had been given a day's holiday
and no one had been there to witness her death. When her

body was discovered, rumors spread fast. Was it murder or suicide? Lady Dudley was known to have been unhappy during her last years. She could have taken her own life.

Dudley was with the Queen at Windsor when the news came. She immediately sent him away from Court until the coroner's inquest was over. Eighteen months of gossip had placed Dudley and even Elizabeth under severe suspicion. The coroner's jury at Cumnor brought in a verdict of accidental death, but no one could link the illness in her breast with a broken neck. Today, Dudley's innocence might have been proved. Modern medical science has shown that cancer of the breast in an advanced stage can cause a spontaneous fracture of the spine. If Lady Dudley had died peacefully in her bed, it might have been possible for Lord Robert to marry Elizabeth. As it was, the circumstances made this impossible.

The shock of the whole affair seemed to bring Elizabeth to her senses. She realized that she would be utterly discredited at home and abroad if she made Dudley her consort. Her reason again took charge of her emotions. Although her love for Dudley continued and he remained an important and powerful favorite in her Court, she gave up all hope of marrying him. "I will have but one mistress in this realm and no master," she declared later. In spite of her many suitors, she kept her word.

Miniature painting of Elizabeth playing the lute. *Right:* Robert Dudley, Earl of Leicester, around 1575.

# 3. Mary, Queen of Scots

Elizabeth had always been curious about her attractive younger cousin, Mary, Queen of Scots, who had spent most of her childhood in France. As a young girl, Mary was said to be gay, pleasure-loving and full of charm. She was tall, with a fine complexion, well-formed features, a high forehead and long, golden-brown hair. In 1558, at the age of fifteen, she was married to the Dauphin, Francis, the fourteen-year-old, sickly son of the King of France.

Mary's mother was a member of the Guise family, one of the most powerful in France, and her father was James V of Scotland. As he died shortly after his daughter's birth, Mary inherited the title of Queen of Scots in her infancy. Through her father, she also had a claim to the English throne. Strict Catholics did not recognize Elizabeth as the rightful heir to the throne because she was a Protestant and her mother had married Henry VIII after divorcing his first wife, who was a Catholic. When Queen Mary of England died, the French King proclaimed his daughter-in-law, Mary, Queen of England and Ireland as well as Scotland. Before Elizabeth had firmly established herself on the throne, she regarded her cousin as a serious rival.

Mary, like Elizabeth, was well educated, a good horsewoman and keen on exercise. They both excelled at the courtly accomplishments of the time and had a particular kind of magnetic charm. The essential differences between them lay in temperament and upbringing. Elizabeth had had to use her wits to survive in a hostile world filled with political intrigue. She had learned to keep her thoughts to herself and to become independent at a very early age. Mary, who was brought up to be Queen of France, had been carefully cossetted, her every need attended to. She had always relied on the advice of others. She was impulsive and lacked the self-discipline and worldly wisdom of her cousin Elizabeth, who was the older by ten years.

Mary's husband, Francis, died shortly after he became King, and Mary found herself a widow at the age of eighteen. Her role as Queen of France was over. She had to return to rule her native Scotland, a country she had left at the age of six. The French regarded Scotland as a cold, barbaric country and the Scots as an unruly, untrustworthy race. The young Queen must have felt certain misgivings as she returned to Scotland after twelve years' absence.

Drawings by the French court painter, Jean Clouet, of Mary, Queen of Scots, at the age of sixteen and of her first husband who reigned briefly as Francis II of France and died in 1560.

Mary had asked Elizabeth for a safe conduct pass so that her ship could sail through English waters without fear of capture. Elizabeth refused her request, saying that she could do nothing until Mary had signed the Treaty of Edinburgh. This was intended to bring about an agreement by England and France for a mutual withdrawal of their military forces from Scotland, but it also stated that Mary renounced all claim to the English throne. Mary would not sign the Treaty and decided to set sail without her cousin's guarantee, risking the consequences. Elizabeth eventually relented, perhaps in the hope of meeting her cousin, but her safe conduct pass arrived too late. Mary had already left.

Elizabeth, at thirty, was still unmarried; her Council was urging her to name a successor to her throne. In many ways, Mary seemed the obvious candidate; her religion was the main stumbling block, but she had already promised the Scots that, although she would remain a Catholic, she would not try to convert Scotland to Catholicism. Elizabeth was far too wily to name her successor openly. She was not going to have a rival claimant to her throne while she lived.

However, as Elizabeth's main fear was that France or Spain might use Scotland as a base from which to invade England, it seemed wise, for the safety of their island, for both Queens to present a common front towards Europe. After Mary's arrival in Scotland, the cousins tried to arrange a meeting. Twice the time and place was fixed but, on both occasions, fate intervened. Bad weather conditions and the state of foreign politics, in turn, prevented their meeting.

Although Elizabeth had not ruled out the idea of marriage, and foreign suitors continued to woo her until she was well on in her forties, she insisted she would marry only for reasons of state, not out of personal choice. In spite of her protestations that she preferred to remain single, the Scottish ambassador was probably closer to the mark when he said to her: "Madam, I know your stately stomach: ye think if ye were married, ye would be but Queen of England, and now ye are King and Queen both; ye may not suffer a commander."

Whatever her real feelings, Elizabeth took a great interest in her cousin's future marriage prospects. Not wanting the Scottish queen to marry a foreign prince, she came up with the surprising proposition that Mary should marry her old suitor, Robert Dudley, Earl of Leicester. Elizabeth knew she

An engraving of Henry, Lord Darnley, and Mary, Queen of Scots, made during the reign of their son, James VI of Scotland and I of England.

38

could trust Leicester to be loyal to her and may also have liked to think that a child of such a marriage could then succeed her. But Mary and Leicester were both unenthusiastic about the idea.

*Darnley and Bothwell*

Instead of Leicester, Mary chose another English subject, like her a direct descendant of Henry VII of England through the female line. He was Henry, Lord Darnley, whom Mary described as "the lustiest and best proportioned long man" she had ever seen.

Darnley's ambitious mother had brought him up to have all the courtly qualities that would enable him to marry well; she sent him to the Scottish Court in Edinburgh at the very time when Elizabeth was encouraging a match between Mary and Leicester. Darnley was well educated, a good dancer and played the lute beautifully. He was tall, like Mary, and had a rather effeminate elegance which matched his boyish face and fair hair.

At nineteen, Darnley was four years younger than Mary when they first met. Their romance blossomed when he fell ill at Stirling Castle and Mary often visited his sickbed. She was so infatuated with her patient that she failed to notice his deficiencies: he was weak-willed, spoiled by doting parents and easily swayed by others. Like Mary, he acted on impulse and did not have the strength of character to give her the support she needed. However, it soon became clear that Mary intended to marry Darnley.

Elizabeth was furious when she heard about the proposed marriage. As Darnley was an English subject, she ordered him to return to England, but he defied the order and married Mary on July 29th, 1565. The Scottish lords, led by the Earl of Moray, Mary's half brother, were also against the marriage; there were long-standing feuds between Scottish clans and Darnley's family, which was a center of Catholic intrigue in England. In addition, he was known to be arrogant and drunken. The Scottish nobles planned a rebellion based on promises of assistance from England. Elizabeth was quite prepared to send the rebels money but she would not provide them with military support. Without English reinforcements, the rebel army faded away.

Mary soon began to realize the true nature of the husband for whom she had sacrificed the goodwill of Elizabeth and her own nobles. Darnley showed himself to be ambitious, petty-minded and disloyal. He did not want the responsibility of kingship and was not interested in the process of government. Nevertheless, he was angry that he had not been granted the crown matrimonial, which would have made him as powerful as his wife and enabled him to remain the ruling King of Scotland if he outlived her. He had no real authority, and as Mary's disillusionment with him became more obvious, he grew bitter and disloyal.

Darnley was easily persuaded that his wife's loss of interest could be explained by her attachment to her little Italian secretary, David Riccio. Though Riccio was small and unattractive, Mary enjoyed his company. Mary was by now pregnant and it was rumored that the baby was Riccio's child. The rumor was probably spread by the discontented Scottish lords who were jealous of the Italian's rise to favor. Darnley was easily convinced that his wife had been unfaithful to him and was quite willing to join the lords in their plan of revenge.

On March 9th, 1566, when Mary was nearly six months pregnant, Darnley and a group of Scottish nobles rushed into her private chamber, where she was supping with Riccio, her ladies and other attendants. They took hold of the little Italian, who was clinging desperately to the Queen's skirts, and dragged him to the head of the stairs, just outside Mary's private chambers. He was stabbed to death and his corpse, bleeding from over fifty dagger wounds, was flung down the winding staircase.

David Riccio, Mary's secretary, who was murdered in 1566, and (*right*) a miniature of James Hepburn, Earl of Bothwell, who became Mary's third husband. Mary divorced him in 1570, and he died in captivity in Denmark in 1578.

Mary, horrified at this butchery, was certain that Darnley was also threatening her life. Always outstandingly brave and resourceful in a crisis, she won over her weak-willed husband and persuaded him to escape with her from Holyrood Palace, in the belief that the rebellious nobles were

planning to imprison her. As the legitimate Queen, she still had the support of some loyal Scottish nobles, and soon men were flocking to aid her against the rebels. Nine days after the murder which had forced her to flee from Edinburgh, she was able to re-enter the city victoriously at the head of 8,000 men and re-establish herself on the throne. Her faltering relationship with her husband had now reached breaking point, but she bided her time until the birth of her son, James, on June 19th, 1566.

Elizabeth was asked to be godmother to the child and relations between the two queens grew warmer again. Elizabeth was also pleased that the pro-English Earl of Moray had returned to favor.

During the crises that followed Mary's marriage, one of her most able and loyal supporters had been James Hepburn, Earl of Bothwell, a man who had a reputation as a womanizer and whose brash behavior had made him unpopular with his fellow courtiers. Despairing of her weak, vacillating husband, Mary turned for help and advice to the well-educated and widely-travelled Bothwell.

After the baptism of her child, Mary began to consider with her councillors how to rid herself of her impossible husband. No immediate solution could be found, and the matter was left in their hands when Mary went to visit her husband in Glasgow, where he was ill, probably with syphilis. She persuaded him to return with her to Kirk o' Field in Edinburgh. There she often slept in the room below his. However, on Sunday, February 9th, 1567, she had to leave him suddenly to attend a wedding masque at Holyrood House, a few miles away. At two o'clock the following morning, a violent explosion blew Kirk o' Field to pieces. Darnley's body was found in the grounds. It was later rumored that he had been strangled – that something had aroused his suspicions and he had been trying to escape in his nightshirt when he was caught and killed. He died before he reached his twenty-first birthday.

Although Bothwell was the main suspect, Mary took no steps to bring him to justice. Elizabeth was horrified and wrote to her immediately. Remembering her bitter experience when Leicester's wife, Amy Robsart, was found dead in mysterious circumstances, Elizabeth wrote a sound letter of advice:

"Oh Madam! I would not do the duty of a faithful cousin and affectionate friend if I thought more of pleasing your ears than saving your honor. I will not conceal from you

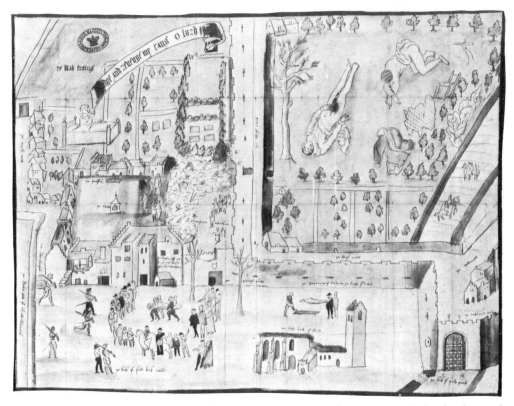

A sketch that was sent to William Cecil in London summing up the scene after the murder of Darnley. The ruins of Kirk o' Field are in the center, with the bodies of Darnley and his servant in the garden, top right, and the bodies being carried away at the bottom. At the top left is the baby Prince James calling from his cradle, 'Judge and avenge my cause, O Lord.'

what most people are saying: that you will look through your fingers at revenge for this deed, and that you have no desire to touch those who have done you such pleasure; as though the deed had not been committed without the murderers knowing they were safe ... I exhort you, I counsel you, I beg you to take this event so to heart that you will not fear to proceed even against your nearest."

Mary ignored this advice and continued to favor Bothwell. Eventually he was given a show trial which was so unconvincing that one wit commented: "Bothwell was not cleansed of the crime, but, as it were, washed with cobbler's blacking."

On April 24th, less than three months after her husband's murder, Mary was abducted by Bothwell as she rode with a small escort from the royal palace at Stirling to Edinburgh. He carried her off to Dunbar Castle, on the coast, where, it was said, he raped her. The Protestant Church pronounced Bothwell an adulterer and granted his wife a divorce. Twelve days later Bothwell and Mary returned to Edinburgh. They were married according to Protestant rites on May 15th, 1567. With this marriage, Mary sacrificed both her honor and the love of her people, who were horrified that their

Queen had married her husband's possible murderer. Thus there was popular support for the many lords who rose against Bothwell. With her forces severely depleted, Mary delivered herself up to the rebel army in order to obtain the release of Bothwell, who had been taken prisoner. The rebel soldiers shouted: "Burn her, burn the whore. She is not worthy to live." And as she was taken along the road to Edinburgh, people cried out: "Kill her! Drown her!" Too late, Mary may have regretted not taking her cousin's advice. Because Elizabeth knew the wisdom of nurturing her popularity, she never lost her people's support.

Mary was imprisoned in the island castle of Loch Leven and forced to abdicate in favor of her baby son, James. Still resourceful and courageous, she escaped in 1568 and managed to raise an army. When her troops were defeated at Langside, she fled to England for safety, arriving in her cousin's country with nothing but borrowed clothes and a handful of faithful followers. Elizabeth, as one of her subjects commented, now had "the wolf by the ears."

*Mary in England*   Throughout Mary's troubles in Scotland, Elizabeth had supported her, not wishing to encourage rebellious subjects against an anointed queen. But now that Mary was in her hands, what was Elizabeth to do with her? William Cecil advised against her coming to Court, for fear that she might stir up the English Catholics. Also, if England were openly to support the fugitive Scottish Queen, Scotland might turn to France for help. Mary was therefore kept in the North of England in the custody of landowners whom Elizabeth trusted. Even so, Catholics were soon flocking to pay their respects to the young Scottish Queen, and many were won over to her cause.

Mary wrote over twenty letters begging Elizabeth for a personal interview, but she was told this was not possible until she was cleared of all complicity in her husband's murder. This excuse gave Elizabeth time to pursue her policy of mediating between the lords and their Queen in order to find a way of restoring Mary to her throne. If Mary could be returned to Scotland as Queen under the careful surveillance of her pro-English nobles, Elizabeth would have extracted herself neatly from a difficult situation. Meanwhile the Earl of Moray was ruling Scotland as Regent to the one-year-old James.

In spite of Mary's protestations that, as a queen, she could have no other judge but God, an inquiry into Darnley's murder took place at York at the beginning of October 1568. Elizabeth insisted that Mary was not to be condemned as guilty. The aim of the inquiry was to consider the conduct of Moray and his party towards Mary and judgment could only be given against them. While Elizabeth hoped that this might lead to the restoration of Mary to her throne, Moray was determined to prove Mary guilty and unfit to rule. The proceedings consequently came to nothing and Elizabeth had them transferred to Westminster in London where she could supervise them more closely. Moray now succeeded in turning the inquiry into a trial concerning Mary's part in her husband's death. As proof of her guilt, he produced the Casket Letters, which were supposed to be letters from Mary to Bothwell that had been stored in a little silver casket. Mary insisted that the letters were forgeries. Their main point in the inquiry was to prove that Mary and Bothwell were lovers before Darnley's death and that together they had plotted his murder. Had the letters been genuine, they would undoubtedly have proved Mary's guilt, but no verdict was brought against her and the inquiry petered out. Moray returned to Scotland to continue his rule as Regent and Mary was left a prisoner, although no crimes had been proved against her.

In this predicament, Mary turned to plots and intrigues. As a Catholic queen with a claim to the English throne, she became a figurehead for the Catholic cause in England.

The first plan was to marry Mary to England's most powerful duke, the Duke of Norfolk, a scheme which Norfolk denied when he was questioned by Elizabeth. Never-

The small silver casket which contained the letters said to be from Mary to Bothwell.

theless he was imprisoned in the Tower of London. Other Catholics were also involved in Mary's cause. The earls in the North raised an army. On November 14th, 1569, they entered Durham Cathedral, where they destroyed the books and the communion table and restored the Catholic Mass. Catholics elsewhere were doing the same. The rebel army marched south towards Mary, who was confined at Tutbury Castle in Staffordshire. At York, however, they turned back, not daring to go farther as the people in the South and the Midlands were loyal to Elizabeth. Large numbers of royalist troops soon dispersed the rebels. Most of the leaders fled to Scotland but some six hundred of their followers were hanged. When news of the rebellion reached Rome, the Pope denounced Elizabeth as a pretender to the throne so that her Catholic subjects could give their allegiance to Mary.

In January 1570, Moray was assassinated in Scotland and Elizabeth lost her main supporter among the Scottish lords. The rebel earls who had escaped over the border were stirring up trouble, and France and Spain were urging that Mary be reinstated on her throne. Although her cousin's presence in England had set off a train of events that was upsetting the peace of her reign, Elizabeth knew that there was no easy solution.

To safeguard her own interests, Elizabeth demanded that Mary's son, James, be sent to England as a hostage before she returned Mary to Scotland. Negotiations began again between Elizabeth, Mary and the Scottish lords, but they were interrupted by the disclosure of another plot.

*Fatal plots*    In 1571, Ridolfi, an Italian banker based in London, organized a harebrained scheme that involved an invasion of England from the Netherlands by Philip II's general, the Duke of Alva. He also managed to secure the support of the Pope in Rome. With this international backing, he hoped to take Elizabeth prisoner and restore the Catholic faith in England and Scotland, probably under the joint rule of Mary and the Duke of Norfolk, who had by then been released from the Tower and placed under restraint in his house. In spite of his promises to have no more dealings with Mary, he unwisely became involved in Ridolfi's plans. William Cecil, who now had the title of Lord Burghley, found out all the details of the plot and particularly of Norfolk's part in it.

The Duke of Norfolk was brought before his peers on a charge of treason and found guilty. He was the first peer in

Elizabeth's reign to be condemned to death. The chief nobleman of the realm, he was well liked and everyone was moved by his fate, most of all the Queen, who was related to him. She kept postponing the task of signing his death warrant and eventually signed it only under pressure.

After the Ridolfi plot, Elizabeth placed Mary under much closer restraint. Elizabeth stopped being careful of her cousin's honor and even permitted the publication of a tract telling the story of Mary, Darnley and Bothwell, as Moray and his party had told it. Parliament felt still more vindictive towards the Scottish Queen. Many of its members wanted to accuse her of treason, but Elizabeth would not let them do so. She was not prepared to have Mary executed. A bill was passed that took away any claim to the English throne that Mary might consider herself to possess and to make the pressing of any such claim a treasonable offense. If Mary plotted against the Queen in future, she could be tried by English peers.

In 1584, when Catholic intrigues against Elizabeth were at their height, the Council drew up the unjust Bond of Association, which meant that Mary could be executed if anyone plotted to place her on the throne, whether or not she was personally involved. During the same year, Elizabeth re-opened negotiations for her cousin's restoration to the Scottish throne, showing remarkable persistence and optimism. These negotiations dragged on rather inconclusively, the main difficulty being that Mary's son, James, now eighteen years old, did not want to share the throne with his mother, whom he had not seen since he was a baby.

In despair, Mary started plotting again. Sir Francis Walsingham, who organized a secret service network, guessed that another plot was forming and devised a clever means of disclosing it. By bribing Mary's agents, he managed to persuade her to use a secret means of smuggling in and sending out her correspondence from Chartley, a house twelve miles away from Tutbury, where she was imprisoned. The letters were packed in a waterproof case and slipped through the bung-hole of a beer barrel. They were delivered in the full barrels and went out in the empties. But on their way in or out of Mary's apartments, Walsingham had them removed, decoded and copied before they were sent on to their destination. In this way, Walsingham soon discovered the facts about the Babington conspiracy.

Anthony Babington, a wealthy young Derbyshire gentleman, and a small group of young men plotted to kill the

Queen as a first step towards putting Mary on the throne. They wrote to tell Mary the details of their plan: six of the conspirators were going to murder Elizabeth while the others came to rescue Mary; they also hoped that the Spanish would invade England. They were, however, very indiscreet and Babington even commissioned a painter to draw portraits of them all before putting the plan into action "as a memorial of so worthy an act".

Walsingham found out their names and rounded up the conspirators. When the plot was revealed, the citizens of London rejoiced that their Queen had been saved. On September 20th, 1586, Babington and six of his fellow plotters were drawn through the streets of London on hurdles. Each received the full traitor's death: being hung on a high scaffold, cut down while still alive and having his entrails pulled out before his eyes.

Mary's position was now critical. However much she insisted that, as a queen, she could be judged only by God, she eventually consented to appear before 36 peers of the realm. Charged with treason and fighting for her life, she defended herself well. Some of the peers were greatly moved

Elizabeth I, painted by
Nicholas Hilliard.

by her speech. She had, after all, come to England trusting
in her cousin's help and, instead, had been kept a prisoner
for many years. She was unwell and bowed down with the
cares of her confined existence. Except for her attendants,
she had no friends or supporters, and even her son made no
real effort to save her. When Mary realized that judgment
had already been passed against her, she determined to die
a martyr to the Catholic faith and concentrated entirely on
her religion.

Elizabeth did not like being cast in the role of executioner.
After all, she had long refused to sacrifice Mary for the sake
of her own safety. When the death sentence was passed on
Mary, Elizabeth delayed signing the warrant.

Mary, however, showed no fear of her coming fate and
spent most of her time in prayer and meditation. It was
Elizabeth who fretted and stormed about her cousin's end.
She even tried to get her secretly murdered rather than

MARIA D·G· SCOTIÆ REGINA, GALLIÆ DOTARIA, MAII 17·1568· AVXILII AB ELISABETHA
PROMISSI SPE ET OPINIONE DESCENDIT IN ANGLIAM·VBI CONTRA IVS GENTIVM, ET
FOEDERIS IVRATI FIDEM, ANNOS VNDEVIGINTI RETENTA, TANDEM HOSPITIS
ELISABETHÆ PARRICIDIO CHRISTI MARTYRIBVS ADDITA, SANGVINIS LI-
BERALITER EFFVSI TESTI- MONIO DEI LEGITIMVM CVLTV,
ET ECCLESIÆ ROMANÆ FIDEM PROFESSA, CORONAM
MERVIT IN CŒLIS, ILLIS TRIBVS ILLVSTRIOREM,
QVARV VSVM VIOLENTE AMISIT IN TERRIS·18·
·FEBRVAR· 1587·

Memorial picture of
Mary, Queen of Scots,
with a legend describing
her as a martyr of the
Roman Catholic church.

appear before the world as the murderer of a fellow queen,
who was also her cousin. It was over three months after
Mary's trial that Elizabeth finally signed the warrant on
February 1st, 1587 for the Queen of Scots' execution. Mary
was not perturbed when she was told on February 7th, that
she was to die the following morning; it was her attendants
who were highly distressed. Mary spent most of the night
in prayer.

At eight o'clock the next day she was led down to the
Hall of Fotheringay Castle. She walked with great dignity,
holding a crucifix and a prayer book. Two rosaries hung at
her waist. She wore a black satin dress with slashed sleeves
that disclosed inner sleeves of purple and a long, white,
lace-edged veil that flowed down behind her. When she
reached the Hall the Protestant Dean of Peterborough tried
to address her, but she waved him aside saying firmly: "Mr.
Dean, I am settled in the ancient Catholic Roman religion

and mind to spend my blood in defense of it." When the executioner asked her, as was the usual custom, to forgive him in advance for bringing about her death, she replied: "I forgive you with all my heart, for now I hope you shall make an end of all my troubles."

She fell on her knees and prayed aloud in Latin. Then her women came forward to prepare her for her beheading. Her black clothes were removed to reveal a red satin bodice trimmed with lace, the neckline cut low at the back; she wore a red velvet petticoat and she put on some red satin sleeves. Thus she approached her death dressed in the color of blood and of martyrdom in the Catholic Church. As she laid her head on the block, she showed no sign of fear and continued praying out loud. Her lips were still moving when her severed head was held up by the executioner, who cried out "God save the Queen." At this moment, the head fell away from its long auburn tresses. Mary had been wearing a wig, and her own hair was quite grey and cropped close to her head. The spectators remained stunned and silent at this sad sight. Only the Dean of Peterborough remembered to call out: "So perish all the Queen's enemies." Mary was 44 when she died.

When Elizabeth heard the news of her cousin's death, she went into a rage, protesting that she had not intended the warrant to be dispatched to Fotheringay. She rebuked her councillors, and only Cecil was bold enough to point out that such play-acting would do little to impress the rest of Europe, where Mary was soon to be hailed as a martyr.

Once the Catholic cause in England lost its figurehead, it lost its strength. There were no more rebellions. Elizabeth again had a peaceful and united kingdom, but she always regretted the price she had had to pay for it.

The execution of Mary, Queen of Scots, depicted by a Dutch artist of the time.

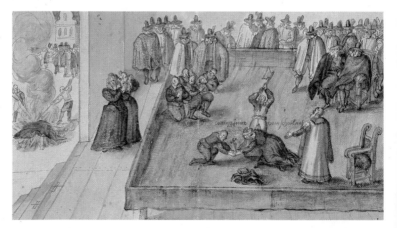

# 4. The Armada and After

The foreign invasion that Mary, Queen of Scots, had so long hoped for was attempted in 1588, the year after her death. Philip II of Spain, infuriated by the pillaging of his trading vessels by English seamen, by Elizabeth's interference in the Netherlands and by the execution of Mary, a Catholic queen, was finally spurred into action.

Elizabeth was still short of money and one of her main reasons for disliking war was the enormous cost of all the necessary men, weapons, ships and supplies. Her courtiers would also be less under her control on the battlefield than they were at Court. Elizabeth tried to avoid becoming entangled in foreign wars by carefully maintaining the balance of power and playing off nations, particularly France and Spain, which she feared most, against each other. Meanwhile she did everything in her power to weaken these countries by indirect means. She secretly encouraged privateering and heaped rewards on adventurers such as Walter Raleigh, Francis Drake and Martin Frobisher, who robbed Spanish trading vessels and brought her back a large part of their

Map of the world as it was known in the late 16th century, published by the Dutch cartographer Abraham Ortelius in his *Theatrum Orbis Terrarum* (1570). By this time, adventurous English mariners were bringing back great wealth from the New World across the Atlantic.

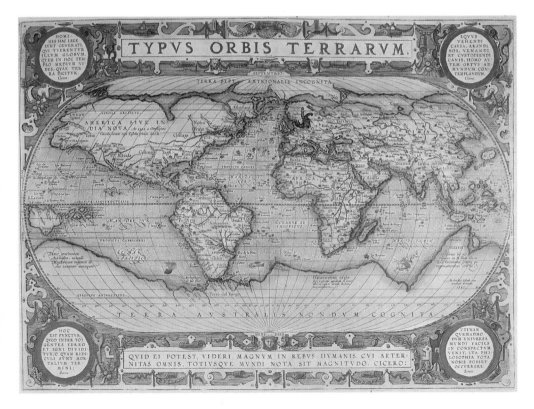

booty. She also allowed them to search for wealth in the New World, America, which the Spaniards considered to be part of their empire. Raleigh, who was handsome, intelligent and witty, a fine example of Elizabethan gallantry, became a great favorite at Court. He was well known for his daring exploits against the Spaniards, but Elizabeth enjoyed his company so much that she refused to let him go on many of the expeditions that he helped to organize. Instead, she gave him lands, money and titles and was delighted by his elegant flattery. It was only when he fell out of favor that he was allowed to go on another expedition to prove his love for her.

The Spaniards were angry at the exploits of the English seamen. Philip II was still more furious when he discovered that much of this stolen wealth was going to finance the Protestant rebels in the Netherlands, which he was trying to incorporate into his Catholic empire. As Elizabeth did not want an open war with Spain, she refused to take up the cause of the Dutch rebels officially. Instead, she sent troops and money to help with their campaigns, and had even, at the age of 45, thought of marrying the Duc d'Alençon, younger brother of the French king and a leader of the Dutch rebels. She probably thought that if Philip were busy trying to keep his own empire under control he would have less time and money to invade England. She also wanted to remain the great figurehead of the Protestant cause.

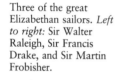

Three of the great Elizabethan sailors. *Left to right:* Sir Walter Raleigh, Sir Francis Drake, and Sir Martin Frobisher.

The Duc d'Alençon at the age of 31, from a painting by Jean Clouet.

Elizabeth I, painted by an unknown artist around 1585.

It was not surprising, then, that when Philip, an ardent Catholic, had been asked to cooperate in the Babington conspiracy to put Mary, Queen of Scots, on the English throne, he felt that the time had indeed come to end the rule of the heretical English Queen. He was not aware that the conspiracy had already been exposed, and his hopes of success set Spanish ports astir in 1586 with preparations for the Armada, the largest and most powerful fleet of ships in the whole of Europe.

The English did not have the same financial resources as the Spaniards but they had some exceptionally skilled seamen and their ship designs were more advanced. Instead of building towering, three-decker ships like the Spaniards, they made smaller, lighter boats that could sail close to the wind and were easy to maneuver. They were also longer and could carry more guns. These were put to the test in 1587 when Drake set out with a small, carefully chosen squadron to destroy the Spanish fleet in their own ports before they

The English fleet fighting
the Spanish Armada.

assembled to invade England. He sailed right in to Cadiz harbor, burned a large number of Spanish ships, which were loaded with provisions, and succeeded in getting back to England unharmed. The expedition proved that the low English ships with their long range guns were more than a match for the Spanish galleons. On his way Drake made further raids into Portugal, captured a Spanish trading vessel filled with treasure and returned in triumph. Because of Drake's efforts, the Spanish invasion had to be delayed until the summer of 1588, when the Armada finally set sail for England, hoping that they would be joined by the Duke of Parma's forces from the Netherlands. Tradition has it that Drake was playing bowls when the Armada was first sighted in the English Channel and that he calmly finished his game before boarding ship.

Elizabeth, too, appeared to be confident throughout the preparations for the invasion. She firmly believed that her countrymen, including the Catholics, would give her support and so they did. Unlike Philip, she had taken care to conserve her resources, and she used all her wits to raise funds for the war. Spurred on by her sense of national pride, the gentry provided both men and money. She never doubted that her country would succeed. When the news reached the Queen that the two fleets had met, Robert Cecil wrote of her reaction: "It is a comfort to see how great magnanimity her Majesty shows, who is not a whit dismayed."

As the Armada approached her shores, Elizabeth rode down to Tilbury to address her troops there. She appeared before them like an "Amazonian empress," riding on a white horse, wearing a white velvet dress beneath a silver breastplate. She was bareheaded, and a page carried her helmet before her on a white cushion while another held the reins of her horse. She inspected her men and called out: "Lord bless you all!" as they fell on their knees and prayed for her. The following day she gave one of her most famous speeches:

"I know I have the body of a weak and feeble woman, but I have the heart and stomach of a king, and of a king of England too, and think foul scorn that Parma or Spain, or any prince of Europe should dare to invade the borders of my realm; to which, rather than any dishonor shall grow by me, I myself will take up arms, I myself will be your general, judge, and rewarder of every one of your virtues in the field."

Meanwhile, Drake cunningly drove the Spaniards up the Channel before Parma's fleet could reach them. The heavy Spanish vessels were helpless against the low, fast-moving English boats with their long-range cannons. The Spaniards were unable to get near enough to the English ships to board them, because of the gunfire, but their own guns were too high up to hit back. In desperation, the Armada retreated to Calais to wait for Parma's fleet but the English sent fire ships, loaded with tar, among them to scatter the Spanish

Fire ships are launched by the English against the Spanish Armada.

The Armada Portrait of Elizabeth I. Behind the idealized picture of the Queen in all her splendour are scenes of the English fleet sailing against the Spaniards and the Armada being wrecked by storms.

ships. Empty of crew, with their sails set, these floating torches bore down on the Spaniards who fled in terror and confusion.

The Spaniards decided to return to Spain by the North Sea, sailing right around the British Isles. The English fleet pursued them as far as Scotland and then returned home victorious, while the Spanish continued north to face storm and shipwreck. England had not lost a single ship or more than a hundred men in action, although problems in obtaining fresh food had resulted in many deaths from disease. Another casualty of the Armada was Leicester. He had left the camp at Tilbury a sick man, probably dying from cancer of the stomach. A week before his death he wrote a letter to Elizabeth. She kept it for the rest of her life in a jewel-box in her bedroom.

After the defeat of the Spanish, there was great jubilation and rejoicing throughout the country. There were three days of tilting, bear-baiting and cock-fighting. Finally, Elizabeth

Probably a more realistic portrait of Elizabeth in middle age.

attended a special service of thanksgiving at St. Paul's Cathedral. She travelled in a chariot drawn by two white horses, with her throne supported by four pillars. At the west door of the Cathedral, she fell on her knees and prayed out loud before the people.

At 55, the Queen was now the symbol of the country's triumph. In public, she was more than ever adored and praised by her people but in private she had to face up to the loss of Leicester and to the coming of old age.

*Elizabeth and Essex*

As Elizabeth gradually lost her old councillors and favorites through death or illness, she began to turn to the young men at her Court. Though she still had surprisingly good health for her age, Elizabeth was no longer attractive to the ambitious young men at Court. The new generation looked upon the game of courtly love as a means of gaining favor. Robert Cecil who, with Elizabeth's full approval, was being trained to take over from his father, Lord Burghley, soon

57

became adept at courtly compliments and gallantries. Small and misshapen, he was known at Court as "the hunchback," but his great aptitude for politics gave him an advantage over his more attractive competitors.

Elizabeth sought a replacement for Leicester among the good-looking noblemen of the Court; the obvious choice was his stepson, the dashing Earl of Essex, Robert Devereux. His natural father had died fighting in Ireland and his widowed mother, the beautiful Lettice Knollys, had then married Leicester, in spite of the Queen's displeasure. Elizabeth invariably resented her old favorites marrying. Essex had been brought up in the household of Lord Burghley, where he had been educated with Robert Cecil. However, Burghley's ability at shrewd statecraft had not left its mark on Essex as it had on his son, Robert. Essex was a much bolder, more flamboyant figure than Robert Cecil, but lacked the self-discipline and worldly wisdom to deal with the complexities of Court life. He underrated his Queen, believing that she was an old woman who could easily be won over to suit his purposes.

When he first appeared at Court, in 1587, Essex was nineteen, with a fine figure and striking good looks. He had already earned himself a reputation as a brave soldier and soon found favor with the Queen. One observer at Court noted: "There is nobody near her but my Lord Essex; and at night my Lord is at cards at one game or another, so that he cometh not to his lodgings till the birds sing in the morning."

Elizabeth was not blind to the faults of her new favorite, but she hoped that, in time, she would be able to tame his wildness and turn him into a responsible leader of men. Essex was only too keen for the fame and glory that leadership would bring him. He constantly begged the Queen to allow him to take part in military campaigns, but she kept him at Court. Eventually, in 1589, the year after the Armada, he slipped away, against her will, and took part in a disastrous expedition to Portugal. Drake, who was in charge of the fleet, hoped to incite the Portuguese to rise against Philip of Spain. He planned to destroy the Spanish fleet and help bring about Philip's downfall. Elizabeth was furious that Essex had gone and more angry still when the sadly depleted force came home unsuccessful and empty-handed. She had invested £20,000 in the campaign and had hoped that they would return with booty that would help pay for the enormous cost of the defeating of the Armada.

Lettice Knollys, mother of the Earl of Essex and second wife of the Earl of Leicester.

She was right to distrust Essex's ability for leadership. Although brave, he was hopelessly irresponsible and tended to treat military campaigns more like field sports than serious enterprises. After the expedition to Portugal, he won his way back to favor and, in 1591, he was allowed by the Queen to lead a small army into Brittany to support the French against Spain; Elizabeth was determined not to allow the Spanish army to establish itself on the north coast of France, within striking distance of England. Characteristically, he got led astray from his task and amused himself instead with rash ventures of his own until the Queen, in a rage, called him home.

In spite of his blatant acts of disobedience, his looks and charm always restored him to favor. Even his marriage, which often proved the downfall of royal favorites, did not seriously upset his rise to fame and fortune. Elizabeth continued to grant him honors and riches. Many of the young noblemen, who hoped to follow him into battle, looked upon Essex as their hero. His popularity with the common people was also remarkable, and his friends warned him not to flaunt this too openly if he wanted to stay in favor with the Queen.

Robert Cecil moved quietly up the political ladder, but Essex made constant demands upon the Queen for key positions in the government for himself and his followers. When these were not granted he sulked like a spoiled child,

Robert Devereux, Earl of Essex. *Right:* Robert Cecil, son of Lord Burghley, painted in 1602. Cecil was made Earl of Salisbury by James I.

yet Elizabeth continued to tolerate his tantrums. One courtier said of Essex: "I know but one friend and one enemy my Lord hath; and that one friend is the Queen and that one enemy is himself."

In 1597, Elizabeth sent Essex to destroy the new Armada that Philip was gathering together in Ferrol on the north coast of Spain. Instead, he went off in search of Spanish treasure ships, and it was only bad weather that prevented Philip's new fleet from reaching England. Essex pressed for war. He even went so far as to launch a public appeal for war against Spain which went directly against Government protocol. The result was a fierce argument during which the Queen struck Essex across the face. It was the first time in forty years that she had used physical violence against one of her councillors. Essex, furious at receiving a blow from a woman, reached for his sword, but others, rushing between him and the Queen, dragged him from the room. Instead of apologizing, Essex wrote Elizabeth an indignant letter that was ominously rebellious in tone: "What, cannot princes err?" he asked. "Cannot subjects receive wrong? Is an earthly power or authority infinite? Pardon me, pardon me, my good Lord, I can never subscribe to these principles."

Elizabeth now treated her former favorite with great caution. To regain favor, Essex took the desperate step of offering to subdue the Irish. Ireland had defeated many great men's reputations, and no one wanted the task of dealing with it. As most of the country had remained Catholic, in violation of English law, Elizabeth feared that France or Spain might use it as a military base. The power of the English overlords in Ireland was being challenged by a dar-

Essex's expedition was only one of a number of attempts under Elizabeth to subdue the Irish. This engraving from *The Image of Irelande* by John Derrick (1581) shows an earlier army under Sir Henry Sidney.

ing and competent leader of the native Irish tribesmen called Hugh O'Neill, Earl of Tyrone. It was Tyrone that Essex was sent to subdue. Elizabeth provided him with the largest and best equipped army that she had ever raised for a military expedition. It was a great drain on her dwindling financial resources, but she wanted Tyrone beaten once and for all. Essex's popularity attracted large numbers of young men eager to follow him into battle. However, he began to get cold feet about the whole project, but as his reputation depended upon the success of the enterprise, he knew that there was now no turning back.

He decided to delay his confrontation with Tyrone for as long as possible. When he arrived in Ireland with his troops in April 1599, he decided to postpone the main operation of attacking Tyrone in Ulster until June. He made the lame excuse that by then there would be sufficient grass and cattle available to feed the army. Meanwhile he led some rather aimless campaigns in the provinces of Leinster and Munster. He had still achieved nothing by July, and he had already wasted the greater part of his troops and provisions. Elizabeth remarked bitterly that she was paying him about £1,000 a day to go on progress. Her scornful letters made Essex's fear of failure grow more intense. It was not until September that he finally confronted Tyrone's forces. After a show battle, he met Tyrone on September 7th, at a ford and had a private talk with him. They came to an agreement between themselves, which was never fully disclosed to anyone else. It was rumored that the two made a deal that Essex should have England and Tyrone Ireland. Essex made peace with Tyrone without imposing any of the conditions that Elizabeth had laid down. All Essex wanted was to get back to England and tell his version of the story to the Queen before anyone else in his army could do so. Leaving his troops in Ireland, he returned with a small force to England and went straight to Court.

Ignoring all the usual protocol, he burst straight into the Queen's bedroom, unannounced. He arrived to find his Sovereign being dressed. He must have seen her as no male courtier had ever done before: without her finery, jewels, make-up or elaborate coiffure. Unsure whether Essex had arrived with a hostile armed force, which could at that moment have been surrounding her palace, Elizabeth received him gracefully and disguised her fears so well that Essex thought he had been forgiven. She remained pleasant and friendly until she was able to measure her own strength against his. When she discovered that Essex had only a small force which he had left in London before hurrying to Court, the Queen had him committed to his room. He was then put into the custody of a fellow councillor, Lord Keeper Egerton. While in Egerton's care, Essex fell ill. In spite of everything, the Queen showed pity on him and sent him her doctor. She wanted him to stand trial in the Star Chamber, the highest court in the land, but her ministers dissuaded her, as they feared the reaction of the people, who were still very much in favor of Essex. By March, he had recovered enough from his illness to be sent back to his own house under the care of a keeper. In June, he was brought before a special commission of councillors but they were given instructions not to charge him with disloyalty. He duly showed repentance and submission. By August, he was free to go anywhere except to Court.

Out of favor and short of money, Essex began to feel desperate about his position. His main source of income came from the lease of the customs on sweet wines, which meant that all English wine merchants had to pay him dues. The lease was granted to him as a royal favor but the Queen failed to renew it, probably intending to teach Essex a lesson. Resentful and hounded by creditors, Essex turned to thoughts of revenge. Gathering other rebellious young men around him, he formed a plot and, on Sunday, February 8th, 1601, rode with an armed band of about two hundred men in the hope of taking possession of the Court, the Tower and the City of London.

Elizabeth, who was probably warned in advance of the rising, remained undaunted. She knew her subjects would remain loyal to her. Although she was now a childless old woman and Essex was a dashing young man, the people were not swayed. When, on Robert Cecil's orders, a herald appeared in the City proclaiming Essex to be a traitor, even his most ardent admirers melted away, and he had to beat a hurried retreat to his house, where he was besieged and taken prisoner by the Queen's men.

A week later, Essex was brought to trial before his peers. When he had been found guilty and condemned to the traitor's death, he spoke out in the manner of the brave soldier that had first won the people's hearts: "I think it fitting," he said, "that my poor quarters, which have done her Majesty true service in divers parts of the world, should now at the last be sacrificed and disposed of at her Majesty's pleasure."

A portrait from around 1600 of an elderly Elizabeth with the figures of Time and Death.

Afterwards, in the Tower, however, he stopped behaving so nobly and made a full confession, sparing none of his friends and even incriminating his own sister. It was not until the day of his execution, February 25th, 1601, that Essex, at the age of 34, was tamed at last. It was reported that "he acknowledged, with thankfulness to God, that he was thus justly spewed out of the realm."

*Final years*

In the first years of the 17th century, Elizabeth urgently needed to raise money. The Spaniards were threatening to take over Ireland and had already landed some troops there. Elizabeth realized that she would have to provide more resources for Lord Mountjoy, who had taken over Essex's job in Ireland and was gradually succeeding in subduing the Irish.

However, she was also confronted with an angry and hostile Parliament. The House of Commons were not prepared to grant any money until they had sorted out their grievances over the question of monopolies. The Sovereign

63

had the exclusive privilege, which could then be conferred on others, of selling certain commodities or trading with particular countries. Many politicians were indignant about the unfairness of these monopolies, which led to excessively high prices. Elizabeth, at heart, agreed with them, but the monopolies were useful to her. Some she had given to favorites such as Essex; the rest she kept as a source of income for the Crown.

In 1601, Parliament was determined to see some action taken. A Bill was presented on the subject, and one Member called monopolists "bloodsuckers of the Commonwealth." The House of Commons became so unruly over the issue that Elizabeth agreed to issue a proclamation revoking a large number of monopolies. She decided to give in gracefully and invited all the Members of Parliament to the Palace at Whitehall, where she delivered to them what later came to be known as her Golden Speech. It was the last great speech she was to make to them, and she used all her skills to arouse their loyalty, patriotism and love by telling them with great eloquence how much she cared for her country.

"There will never be a Queen [that will] sit in my seat with more zeal to my country, care for my subjects, and that will sooner with willingness venture her life for your good and safety, than myself. For it is my desire to live nor reign no longer than my life and reign shall be for your good. And though you have had, and may have, many princes more mighty and wise sitting in this seat, yet you never had, nor shall have, any that will be more careful and loving."

It was an emotional moment for a woman, nearing the age of seventy, who was looking back on more than forty years of personal rule. The speech was printed and reprinted during the next two generations, as a testament of what it was to be a caring monarch.

At last, though, Elizabeth's extraordinary youthfulness was beginning to wear thin. Her godson, Sir John Harington, described how she looked a fortnight before the Golden Speech. He wrote that: "She was quite disfavored and unattired, and these troubles waste her much. She disregardeth every costly cover that cometh to the table, and taketh little but manchet and succory potage. Every new message from the City doth disturb her and she frowns on all the ladies."

The loss of Essex and the battles with Parliament were taking their toll, but in 1602, in the last full year of her life, she became reasonably well and happy again. She was delighted by the reception of her Golden Speech and still better pleased by the good news from Ireland that Tyrone's forces had at last been defeated.

She was still able to dance on public occasions and once, in August 1602, she rode 10 miles (16 kilometres), then went out hunting the same day. She also kept up her usual round of Court entertainments, but it became clear by the autumn that her powers were failing. She became more difficult to deal with and less inclined to attend to business. Although she was still handling Irish affairs with great attention, she seemed less interested in everything else. She was also suffering from severe bouts of depression.

It was not until the end of February 1603 that she admitted she was not well and told one of her courtiers that "her heart had been sad and heavy." On March 9th, her doctor reported that she had been ill for nearly a fortnight, "being seized with such a restlessness that though she has no formed fever, she felt a great heat in her stomach, and a continual thirst, which obliged her every moment to take something to abate it, and to prevent the hard and dry phlegm, with which she is sometimes oppressed, from choking her ... she has been obstinate in refusing everything prescribed by her physician during her sickness."

She was equally stubborn about retiring to bed and stayed propped up on cushions, refusing to eat, preoccupied with thoughts of death. When Sir John Harington tried to raise her spirits by telling her a joke, she rebuked him with the warning: "When thou dost feel creeping time at thy gate, these fooleries will please thee less."

Marble head of Elizabeth I from her tomb in Westminster Abbey. Mary, Queen of Scots, is also buried in the Abbey.

Eventually, on March 21st, she was persuaded to go to bed. There, for a while, she felt a little better and called for broth. On the following day, Robert Cecil, the Lord Keeper and the Lord Admiral gathered around her bed. It was said later that, during this interview, Elizabeth finally broke her silence on the question of the succession and indicated that her cousin, King James VI of Scotland, the son of Mary, Queen of Scots, should succeed her. The next day she was visited by a larger body of representatives who hoped to witness her announcement about her successor but they found her incapable of speech. It was said that Cecil asked her to give some sign that King James was her choice and she slowly lifted her fingers together in the form of a crown. Whether the story was true or not, it was certainly useful for Cecil, who had been surreptitiously arranging for James's succession for some time. He had horses ready to take the news of Elizabeth's death to Scotland with all speed.

He did not have long to wait. Elizabeth died soon after midnight on March 24th, 1603. It was a Thursday, the death-day of her father and his other children. A contemporary description of her last moments said: "This morning about three o'clock her Majestry departed this life, mildly like a lamb, easily like a ripe apple from a tree . . . Dr Parry told me he was present, and sent his prayers before her soul; and I doubt not but she is amongst the royal saints in heaven in eternal joys."

Elizabeth I had reigned for 45 years. At 69, she had lived to a greater age than any of her predecessors. Few of her subjects could remember what it was like to have a king on the throne. Elizabeth had lived to prove that a woman on her own could rule a country as well and better than a man. Few reigns have been so glorious.

She had turned England from a small, insignificant country into a world power with a strong sense of its own national character. She had given her subjects comparative peace and prosperity after the turmoil of the previous two reigns. English trade had flourished. The great pioneering voyages to the New World of America and the sea battles against the Spaniards had made English seamanship famous. Her Court had been as impressive as that of her father, Henry VIII, and had become a center for English art and culture. Poets, musicians, dramatists and artists were all patronized by their cultured and intelligent Queen. To many writers of her time, she had also been a great source of inspiration. Gloriana, the Virgin Queen, was immortalized in their works. She became the romantic figurehead for the new sense of patriotism that had been aroused in her subjects. By using all her shrewdness, her political sense and her flair for communicating with her people, Elizabeth made her reign a magnificent era in the history of England.

The funeral of Elizabeth I.

# Chronology

This list of dates gives the main events in the life of Elizabeth I together with some of the many other things not mentioned elsewhere in this book that were happening in the world at the same time. Events in bold type are mentioned in the main text of this book.

1533 **Henry VIII marries Anne Boleyn and is excommunicated by the Pope. Birth of Elizabeth.** Thomas Cranmer appointed Archbishop of Canterbury. Ivan IV (The Terrible), aged 3 becomes Prince of Moscow.

1534 **Henry VIII becomes head of Church in England.** Hans Holbein becomes his Court Painter.

1535 First Bible printed in English.

1536 **Execution of Anne Boleyn.** Death of Catherine of Aragon.

1537 **Birth of Edward (later Edward VI).**

1541 Henry VIII assumes title of King of Ireland. Protestant John Knox begins Reformation in Scotland.

1542 **Birth of Mary, who becomes Queen of Scots** on death of James V of Scotland.

1543 Publication in Basle, Switzerland, of the first great modern scientific work, *De Fabrica Corporis Humani* by Andreas Vesalius, on human anatomy. Death of astronomer Copernicus and publication of his *De Revolutionibus Orbium Celestium* with view of universe in which the Earth is not the centre.

1547 **Death of Henry VIII. Accession of Edward VI.** Michelangelo appointed chief architect of St. Peter's, Rome.

1549 **Execution of Thomas Seymour.**

1551 Publication of first volume of the Swiss Conrad Gesner's *Historia Animalium*, the first modern zoology book.

1553 **Death of Edward VI. Lady Jane Grey is Queen for nine days. Accession of Mary I.** Death of painter Lucas Cranach.

1554 **Sir Thomas Wyatt's rebellion. Execution of Lady Jane Grey. Mary I marries Philip II of Spain.**

1555 Bishops Latimer and Ridley burned at stake.

1556 Archbishop Cranmer burned at stake.

1558 **Calais, last British possession in Europe, lost to French. Death of Mary I. Accession of Elizabeth I. William Cecil appointed Secretary of State. Marriage of Mary, Queen of Scots, to Francis, Dauphin of France (later Francis II).**

1559 **Coronation of Elizabeth I. Treaty of Cateau-Cambrésis.**

1560 **Treaty of Edinburgh. Death of Francis II. Death of Amy Robsart.**

1561 **Mary, Queen of Scots, returns to Scotland.** Birth of philosopher Francis Bacon.

1562 Wars of Religion begin in France. Birth of composer John Dowland.

1563 Thirty-Nine Articles issued defining Anglican faith. Foxe's *Book of Martyrs* published.

1564 Birth of playwrights William Shakespeare and Christopher Marlowe, and astronomer Galileo Galilei. Death of Michelangelo.

1565 **Mary, Queen of Scots marries Henry, Lord Darnley.**

1566 **Murder of David Riccio. Birth of James, later James VI of Scotland and I of England.**

1567 **Murder of Darnley. Earl of Bothwell abducts and marries Mary, Queen of Scots, who is forced to abdicate in favour of James VI.**

1568 **Mary's forces defeated at Langside. She flees to England.** Start of rebellion against Spanish in Netherlands.

1569 **Catholic rebellion in North of England.**

1570 **Assassination of Earl of Moray, Regent of Scotland.** Elizabeth I excommunicated by Pope.

1571 **Ridolfi plot.**

1572 French Protestants massacred on St. Bartholomew's Day. **Execution of Duke of Norfolk.**

1573 Birth of painter Caravaggio.

1574 Richard Burbage opens first theatre in England.

1576 Death of painter Titian.

1577 Sir Francis Drake sets out on first English voyage around the world.

1579 Rebellion in Ireland.

1580 Drake completes round the world voyage. Philip II of Spain invades Portugal. Death of architect Andrea Palladio.

1584 **Bond of Association.** Sir Walter Raleigh sails to Virginia. Assassination of William the Silent, Duke of Orange, leader of the Dutch against the Spanish. Death of Ivan the Terrible.

1585 First English colony in America established at Roanoke Island, Virginia (abandoned 1587). English expedition to Netherlands under Earl of Leicester. Start of war with Spain.

1586 **Babington plot. Trial of Mary, Queen of Scots.**

1587 **Execution of Mary, Queen of Scots. English attack Spanish fleet at Cadiz. Earl of Essex arrives at Court.** Marlowe writes *Tamburlaine*. Claudio Monteverdi writes his first book of madrigals.

1588 **Defeat of Spanish Armada.** Death of painter Veronese.

1589 **Unsuccessful English military campaign in Portugal.** Richard Hakluyt publishes his *Voyages*.

1590 First three volumes of Edmund Spenser's *The Faerie Queene* published.

1591 **Essex leads English expedition to Brittany.**

1594 Death of painter Tintoretto.

1596 Death of Sir Francis Drake.

1597 **Second Spanish Armada turned back by bad weather.** First edition of Francis Bacon's *Essays*.

1598 Deaths of Philip II of Spain and William Cecil, Lord Burghley. End of French Civil War. Henri IV of France issues Edict of Nantes, tolerating Protestants. Publication of *Love's Labour Lost*, first play published under Shakespeare's name.

1599 **Expedition to Ireland led by Essex.** Birth of Oliver Cromwell. Death of Edmund Spenser. Globe Theatre opened with Shakespeare as shareholder.

1601 **Rebellion led by Essex. Execution of Essex. Elizabeth I makes Golden Speech.**

1602 East India Company incorporated in England.

1603 **Death of Elizabeth I. Accession of James VI of Scotland as James I of England: Union of the Crowns.** Foundation of Dutch East India Company.

# Books to Read

This list includes some of the many books in which you can read more about Elizabeth I and her times. Some of them are short and very readable, while others are large and detailed books that you may want to look at in libraries. The names of the British and American publishers and the date of first publication are given after each title. Many of the books have also been published in paperback.

## ELIZABETH I
*Elizabeth I* Jackdaw folder (Cape/Viking)
*Elizabeth I & her Courtiers* Neville Williams (Weidenfeld & Nicolson, 1972) published in US as *Elizabeth I & her Court* (Macmillan Inc.)
*Elizabeth & Leicester* Elizabeth Jenkins (Gollancz, 1961), published in US as *The Biography of Lord Leicester* (Coward McCann)
*Elizabeth the Great* Elizabeth Jenkins (Gollancz, 1958), published in US as *Queen Elizabeth* (Coward McCann)
*Fanfare for Elizabeth* Edith Sitwell (Macmillan/Macmillan Inc., 1946)
*The Queens & the Hive* Edith Sitwell (Macmillan/Little, Brown, 1962)
*Queen Elizabeth I* J.E. Neale (Cape/Doubleday, 1934)

## MARY I
*Bloody Mary* Carolly Erikson (Dent/Doubleday, 1978)

## HENRY VIII
*Henry VIII & his Six Wives* Jackdaw folder (Cape/Viking)
*Great Harry* Carolly Erikson (Dent/Doubleday, 1980)

## TUDOR ENGLAND
*The Armada* Jackdaw folder (Cape/Viking)
*The Defeat of the Spanish Armada* Garrett Mattingly (Cape, 1959)
*Elizabethan Citizen* Marjorie Reeves & Paule Hodgson (Then & There series, Longmans, 1961)
*Elizabethan Image* Roy C. Strong (Tate Gallery/Barron's, 1969)
*Elizabeth's Court* Marjorie Reeves (Then & There series, Longmans, 1956)
*Elizabeth's England* David Birt (Longmans, 1981)
*The England of Elizabeth* A.L. Rowse (Macmillan/St Martin's Press, 1950)
*A History of Everyday Things in England: 1500–1799* C.H.B. & Marjorie Quennell (Batsford/Putnam, 1976)
*Tudor England* S. Bindoff (Pelican History of England, Penguin/Viking)
*The Tudors* Christopher Morris (Batsford/Macmillan Inc., 1955)

## MARY, QUEEN OF SCOTS
*Mary, Queen of Scots* Alan Bold (Wayland, 1977)
*Mary, Queen of Scots* Antonia Fraser (Weidenfeld & Nicolson/Delacourt, 1969)
*Mary, Queen of Scots* Roy C. Strong & Julia Trevelyan Oman (Secker & Warburg/Stein & Day, 1972)

# Index

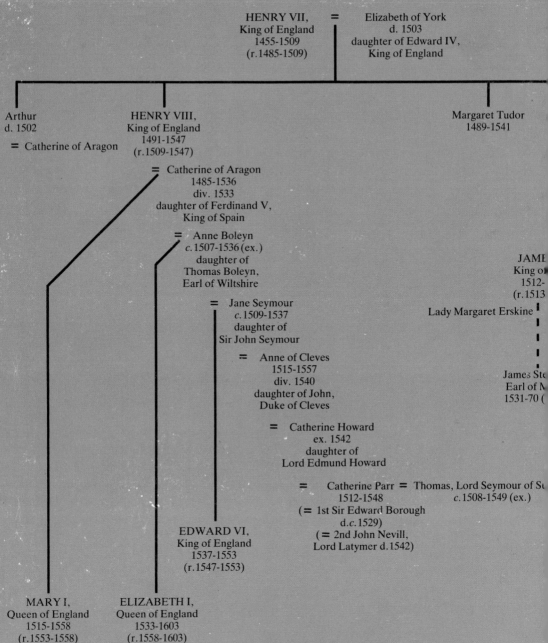

**HENRY VII,** = Elizabeth of York
King of England      d. 1503
1455-1509          daughter of Edward IV,
(r.1485-1509)       King of England

**Arthur**                **HENRY VIII,**                                                    Margaret Tudor
d. 1502                  King of England                                                    1489-1541
= Catherine of Aragon    1491-1547
                         (r.1509-1547)

= Catherine of Aragon
  1485-1536
  div. 1533
  daughter of Ferdinand V,
  King of Spain

= Anne Boleyn
  c.1507-1536 (ex.)                                                            JAME
  daughter of                                                                  King of
  Thomas Boleyn,                                                               1512-
  Earl of Wiltshire                                                            (r.1513

= Jane Seymour                                          Lady Margaret Erskine
  c.1509-1537
  daughter of
  Sir John Seymour

= Anne of Cleves
  1515-1557
  div. 1540                                                                    James Ste
  daughter of John,                                                            Earl of M
  Duke of Cleves                                                               1531-70 (

= Catherine Howard
  ex. 1542
  daughter of
  Lord Edmund Howard

= Catherine Parr = Thomas, Lord Seymour of Su
  1512-1548          c.1508-1549 (ex.)
(= 1st Sir Edward Borough
  d.c.1529)
(= 2nd John Nevill,
  Lord Latymer d.1542)

**EDWARD VI,**
King of England
1537-1553
(r.1547-1553)

**MARY I,**              **ELIZABETH I,**
Queen of England         Queen of England
1515-1558                1533-1603
(r.1553-1558)            (r.1558-1603)

= Philip II,
  King of Spain
  1527-98

# The Tudors and the Stuarts